BLESSED

CATHERINE LABOURÉ

DAUGHTER OF CHARITY
OF SAINT VINCENT DE PAUL

1806—1876

Translated from the French
OF REV. EDMOND CRAPEZ, C. M.

Second Edition

ST. JOSEPH'S, EMMITSBURG, MD.

1933

𝔍mprimatur:

✠ JAMES CARDINAL GIBBONS
Archbishop of Baltimore

Baltimore, March 19, 1918

"O MARY IMMACULATE, COVER ME WITH YOUR VIRGINAL MANTLE AND PRESENT ME TO YOUR DIVINE SON."

Blessed Catherine Laboure

CONTENTS

INTRODUCTION

The life story of every faithful Servant of God is a power for good because example is so much more potent than precept. Such books have been the starting point in holiness for some of the greatest saints, notably St. Augustine, the great Doctor of Hippo, and St. Ignatius Loyola. The humble daughter of St. Vincent de Paul, Venerable Sister Catherine Labouré,* gives us practical lessons in the love of the hidden life which our Lord Himself spent thirty of the precious three and thirty years in teaching men. During almost all her long life as a Daughter of Charity, her days differed from those of thousands upon thousands of her white cornetted Sisters throughout the world only in the greater interior fervor of soul which stamped all her actions with the love of her Divine Spouse and His Immaculate Mother. It was an uninterrupted series of ordinary actions performed extraordinarily well.

*Now Blessed Catherine.

INTRODUCTION

But the secret source of her sanctity gives to the history of her humble career a special and endearing interest, for it was an intense love for the Immaculate Mother of God. This brought its great reward at the very threshold of her life as a Sister in the mission of transmitting to the world one of Mary's most precious gifts to our race. The Miraculous Medal, like the Rosary and the Scapular of Mount Carmel, has wrought wonders for souls everywhere.

The visions of the Immaculate Virgin, and the commission to use the heaven-sent medal for spreading devotion to her under her dearest title, though faithfully accomplished, proved no prejudice to the humble obscurity in which the Venerable Seer lived and died. And yet she was by the devotion which the medal propagated and fostered, an instrument in God's hands for bringing to the Catholic world a fuller realization of the beauty of Mary's immaculate soul, that culminated in the dogmatic promulgation of Pius IX on December the eighth, eighteen hundred fifty-four.

INTRODUCTION

Every client of Mary Immaculate should love the story of Sister Catherine Labouré and her mission. The present record of it, coming from the very spot where the vision was granted, and based on the most intelligent and industrious study of original sources, is sure to do a world of good, and so it is to be hoped that it will spread far and wide.

This translation is the work of an octogenarian Daughter of Charity of Emmitsburg, who in the evening of life gave her hours to this labor of love, when freed by her age from more active duties. God has called her to her reward, but this last work of hers will preach to men confidence in the Help of Christians, whose aid we need so much in these days of storm and stress.

JAMES CARDINAL GIBBONS.

FEAST OF SAINT JOSEPH, 1918.

x

Nihil Obstat:

> Angelus Mariani, S. C. Adv.
> *Sacr. Rit. Congregationis Assessor*

Nihil Obstat;

> P. Meugniot, C. M.
> A. Rougé, C. M.

Imprimatur:

> A. Fiat
> *Superior General*

Imprimatur:

> H. Odelin
> *Vicar General*

Paris, November 7, 1910

DECLARATION OF THE AUTHOR

In obedience to the decrees of Urban VIII, March 13, 1625 and June 16, 1631, I protest that in applying to Sister Catherine Labouré or to others mentioned in this book, attributes restricted by ecclesiastical law, I have used such terms only to prove innocence of life and excellence of virtue, and in regard to the extraordinary events related, I claim to present these facts as sanctioned merely by private judgment without in any way anticipating the authority of Holy Mother Church, in whose obedience I desire to live and die.

LETTER

of

Very Rev. A. Fiat, Superior General

Esteemed Sir and very dear Confrère:

The grace of our Lord be ever with you!

Historical accuracy distinguishes your admirable
treatise, "Venerable Catherine Labouré."* Not imagination but facts, either attested by documents
placed at your disposal, or gathered after diligent
research, guided you in your treatment of her simple and hidden career. Nor is the logical character
of the work in any wise prejudicial to its historical
value. In your anxiety for the truth you have not
concealed the abuses which had glided into the two
families of Saint Vincent, abuses which attracted

* Now Blessed Catherine.

LETTER

the maternal solicitude of the Blessed Virgin whose
beneficent influence operated in their midst so
happy a reform. Still you have handled the matter so judiciously as to present only those features
necessary to reveal both Mary's fidelity to her
promises and the part played by Sister Catherine
in the restoration of the interior spirit. You have
erected an enduring even though modest monument, not so much in honor of the favored Seer as
in honor of the Immaculate Virgin.

This is indeed a manifestation. The pious
Foundress of the Daughters of Charity had besought God to manifest to mankind the sublime
sanctity of the Blessed Virgin that all creatures
might eternally praise her Immaculate Conception.
Appreciating the matchless delicacy of her prayer,
Mary desired, as it were, to emulate its tenderness by electing from the very family of Louise de
Marillac the instrument destined to make her known
and invoked as immaculate in her conception.

It is a manifestation of the exquisite tenderness
of our heavenly Mother. On the occasion of the
first apparition to Catherine Labouré, July 18, 1830,

the Blessed Virgin amid tears of sorrow, foretold that great calamities were about to fall upon society. But this Mother of Mercy unwilling that the little Sister should continue under the strain of grievous apprehension, appears again November twenty-seventh of the same year, holding in her hands and pressing to her heart a terrestrial globe, recommending it to God and deluging it, as it were, with graces obtained by her powerful intercession, graces which radiated from her fingers under the symbol of luminous rays.

It is a most consoling manifestation. Mary seeks to forewarn us that in the evils that afflict us she will be neither afar off nor disinterested. She will pray and cause others to pray. In this we find a hidden announcement of the coming events at Lourdes and other privileged sanctuaries beginning with that of Our Lady of Victory in Paris. This prophetic manifestation reassured Sister Catherine and filled her soul with delight. But how was the favor to be communicated to the children of the Church with the incontestable marks of authenticity? Mary herself reveals the secret: "Have a

medal struck according to the model shown you."
Thus the medal is a manifestation of the solicitude
of Mary for the welfare of mankind, and the num-
berless miracles wrought in favor of those using it,
attest its authenticity.   It is at the same time a
memorial of the Manifestation of 1830, a pledge of
the fidelity of Mary to her promises, and the potent
instrument of her mercy.

However in its form now irrevocably fixed the
medal reproduces only one of the apparitions.   It
shows the Blessed Virgin extending her hands filled
with graces which fall not only on France but on
the entire world and especially on those who invoke
her aid.   Artists of that period were unsuccessful
in reproducing on metal that vision equally prophetic representing the Virgin holding the globe in
her hands and pleading with God for the needs of
humanity.   The Venerable Sister would have preferred this attitude as expressive of our Immaculate
Mother's merciful intervention in our behalf, and
as manifesting more perfectly the character of advocate and dispensatrix of grace.

Some time before her death Sister Catherine

became anxious fearing she had not fully accomplished her mission, had not sufficiently emphasized the honor due to Mary as suppliant, an attitude which she deigned to assume for our consolation. She therefore asked and obtained permission to have a statue constructed on this model. This statue placed on a small altar, on the very site of the apparition, is known under the title of Virgin Most Powerful. Truly powerful is she since by the sole influence of her prayers she disarms the justice of God and obtains mercy for her clients.

You have, esteemed Sir and very dear Confrère, presented in the life of Venerable Catherine Labouré the type of a true Daughter of Charity. Closely united to God, devoted to labor, favored by celestial communications of great and consoling importance, she ever preserved inviolable secrecy regarding her trust. The lifelong object of the predilection of Mary, she still remained unknown, sheltered in obscurity. Truly God bestowed a gift of unsurpassed excellence on the Community by sending us this angelic child. May He and His holy Mother be forever blessed! May we of today profit by the

LETTER

graces this favored child of Heaven solicits for the two families so dear to her during her earthly career!

Receive, esteemed Sir and very dear Confrère, my sincere thanks and cordial appreciation of your work. May the blessing of Heaven attend its publication!

I remain affectionately in the love of Our Lord and His Immaculate Mother,

Your devoted servant

A. Fiat, u. p. o. t. m.

Superior General

Feast of Blessed John Gabriel Perboyre, 1910

XVI

PREFACE

The biography of Sister Catherine Labouré, so favored by the apparitions of 1830, is presented to the Catholic reader as a page of the history of the dogma of the Immaculate Conception.

What especially characterizes this Daughter of Saint Vincent de Paul, known as the "Seer of the Miraculous Medal," is not the remarkable simplicity of a soul, the almost constant recipient of exceptional favors, nor the rare humility which during forty-six years shrouded in silence the secret of her supernatural revelations. No, her prominence is due to the mission intrusted her by God and to her fidelity in its accomplishment.

Now what was the nature of this mission? It centers around the dogma of the Immaculate Conception. A learned theologian who made a profound study of "the dogma and of the Catholic mind" in the nineteenth century, formally declares that the dissemination of the Miraculous Medal was an important factor in preparing the way for the

PREFACE

definition of 1854. The Act of Pius IX undoubtedly gave a fresh impetus to Marian theology and
Father Bainvel represents theologians thenceforth
earnestly adopting various means to place in bolder
relief a prerogative recognized and accepted, if you
will, but for the greater part, ill understood and
taking no definite shape. I refer to the coopera-
tion of Mary in the work of redemption and of the
part assigned her in the distribution of the graces
that come to us from God.

We believe that the Miraculous Medal more
widely circulated, understood in its entire symbolism interpreted by the Manifestation of 1830, will
contribute in its own way to yield the happy result
foreseen by theologians. The biography of Sister
Catherine presented as it is under three aspects, the
preparation, the mission, and its consequences will
develop these ideas. Her childhood and youth at
Fain-les-Moutiers, her vocation as a Daughter of
Charity, the apparitions of 1830 which serve as a
preparation for her peculiar mission: this is the burden of the first three chapters. The fourth chapter
entitled "The Manifestation of the Immaculate

PREFACE

Virgin, November 27, 1830" is by far the most important as it gives the account of this manifestation and determines the nature of the mission of Sister Catherine. The last chapters may be classed under the general heading "Consequences of this Mission," firstly, social consequences, the Miraculous Medal, the growth of the two families of Saint Vincent de Paul, the origin of the Children of Mary; secondly, personal consequences, her life, that of the ideal Daughter of Charity, her death, that of a predestined soul arrived at the degree of perfection appointed by the Most High.

The sources whence we have derived the material for this subject are numerous. In the first place we have studied, utilized and compared one with another, the authentic writings of Sister Catherine. In relating the apparitions we have preserved the texts of the manuscripts altering errors in orthography and punctuation only, giving in parentheses either words apparently omitted by the Seer or an elucidation of her thought. Besides availing ourselves of these fundamental sources of information we have sedulously examined other

PREFACE

authentic documents such as the Canonical Inquiry
of 1836, the various "Notices" published on the
Medal and the many testimonies oral and written
collected at the birthplace of Sister Catherine and
from her Community in Paris.

A decree of the Sacred Congregation of Rites,
signed by His Holiness, Pius X, December 11,
1907, approves the introduction of the cause of
beatification and canonization of Catherine Labouré.
The present effort includes the main lines of this
history presenting a biography at once scientific and
popular.

Such is the aim of this task undertaken through
obedience, aided by highly esteemed collaboration,
and lovingly dedicated to Mary conceived without
sin.

THE AUTHOR

BLESSED CATHERINE LABOURÉ

CHAPTER I

FAIN-LES-MOUTIERS

1806—1824

CATHERINE LABOURÉ was born in the village of Fain-les-Moutiers, in the vicinity of Moutiers-Saint-Jean, in the department of Côte-d'Or. Moutiers recalls the ancient monastery, now in ruins, founded in the fifth century by the holy abbot John. Mabillon gives in the annals of the order of Saint Benedict the authentic origin of the abbey so celebrated in the reformed Congregation of Saint Maur.

An interesting legend relates how Clovis, the first Christian king of France, honored the founder of the old monastery with especial protection. On a certain occasion the king offered to him as much land as mounted on an ass he could traverse in one day. Saint John accepted the terms and thus secured for the abbey the possession of several of the surrounding villages among them Fain-les-Moutiers.

On leaving Moutiers one enters a gently sloping pathway which rising abruptly leads to a tableland the prospect whence discloses an immense horizon and invites the soul to contemplation. At a distance of a half mile nestling among the trees, the dwellings of Fain-les-Moutiers, or Fain as it is familiarly styled, are distinctly seen, the spot where at the dawn of the nineteenth century, a lovely flower of beauty and holiness, the Blessed Catherine Labouré whose life we are about to recount, first saw the light.

No one perhaps has more happily delineated the loveliness of the Burgundian country in the environs of Fain-les-Moutiers than Louis Veuillot. "Under the canopy of a cloudless sky," this eminent Catholic author writes to his sister in 1858, "I traversed four miles of country redolent with new mown hay, listening the while to the song of the lark and the sweet tones of the Angelus bell. Charming indeed are the preparations which usher in the day!"

FAIN-LES-MOUTIERS

"It seemed as if the curtains of night were at first but slightly parted, then daylight made way enveloping earth in the beauty of rosy dawn. Suddenly the graceful curves of the hills were discernible. The trees and fields had cast off their sombre hues and were decked in green and gold. Rosy tinted Aurora now opens her casement and looks out. What a winning countenance! Pale and smiling, aglow yet betraying a tinge of melancholy. A few stars here and there mark her nightly headdress. Then these having fallen to earth are transformed, as it were, into refreshing streams and bright flowers. At length her morning toilet, perfumed by the linden blossom, the delicate elderberry and the new mown hay, is complete. Her breath is fresh and sweet. She comes to me with an invigorating influence which I should delight to share with you in your straightened enclosure of Rue du Bac."

"Brighter grows the dawn. All nature responds. The birds warble songs and bid me learn from them how to make my morning prayers. Yet we are destined to see more than this. Beautiful as it is" continues Veuillot, alluding to a personal sorrow, "we shall hearken to the prayers of the angels, sweeter than the song of birds and in this concert of praise, recognize the voice of our beloved daughter Marie."

In 1830 Sister Catherine Labouré will enjoy the privilege of listening to the voice not of the angels but of their Queen. True she will lack the genius of a Veuillot to portray the supernatural visions nor will she have the talent to depict as he has done, the beauty of the Burgundian sky and the charms of the rosy dawn, still in seeking a type of beauty to describe, the robe and veil of the Immaculate, this child of Fain-les-Moutiers recalling youthful impressions will say, "It was like the rose tint of the early morn."

The birthplace of Blessed Sister Catherine is not far from Montbard, the home village of Aleth the mother of Saint Bernard, nor from Bourbilly that of Saint Jane Frances Frémyot de Chantal. While the parents of Catherine Labouré were not, as is the case of the families of Frémyot and Aleth, of noble extraction, neither were they of the very

4

humble origin usually ascribed to them. The author of the unreliable work "Foules de Lourdes" has devoted some splendid pages to the Seer of Rue du Bac wherein we read:

"At Paris as well as at La Salette and Lourdes the Virgin has selected as her intermediaries country girls unpretending, uncouth and of ordinary capacity. At La Salette and at Lourdes she chooses shepherdesses, Mélanie and Bernadette and at Paris where shepherdesses are not to be found, she culls from among the Daughters of Charity one who had formerly been employed as a servant and farmhand."

The parallel seems ingenious but it is not accurate for Sister Catherine was not, in the common acceptation of the term, a farmhand, though such a condition has nothing degrading about it. Her father Pierre Labouré notwithstanding his descent from one of the most honorable families of the country, cultivated his own land. He was moreover for several years from 1811 to 1815 Mayor of Fain-les-Moutiers, the immediate successor in that office of one of his relatives, Nicholas Labouré.

5

BLESSED CATHERINE LABOURÉ

In his youth the father of our Blessed Sister with a view to embracing the ecclesiastical state, had entered the Seminary, but was constrained, probably by the Revolution, to abandon his clerical studies. It would seem that Providence had other designs over the young man; that his vocation was not to minister at God's altar, but to establish a patriarchal and Christian family that should give a numerous progeny to France and a saint to the Church.

At any rate, two days after the proclamation of the Reign of Terror, June 4, 1793, Pierre Labouré married Louise Madeleine Gontard, a pious young woman of Senailly, parish of Saint Germain, near Moutiers-Saint-Jean. The future mother of Sister Catherine was one of those French women of whom the American author, Orestas A. Brownson writes: "During the darkest days of France, when the religion of the country was abolished, the churches profaned, the clergy put to death, the impious worship of the lewd Venus revived, an immense majority of the women of France kept the faith and preserved intact devotion to the Blessed

6

FAIN-LES-MOUTIERS

Virgin. . . . . . There is ever hope for a nation so long as its women remain pure and true to the faith."

The young couple passed the first years of their married life so blessed by God, at Senailly. From 1794 to 1800 four children were born to them, Hubert, Marie Louise, James and Anthony. Later on at Fain-les-Moutiers, then become their permanent abode, four others, Charles, Alexander, Joseph and Pierre Charles successively brought joy to the family circle. These eight children, the glory and delight of their parents nevertheless necessitated increased labor and anxiety for their maintenance. But Pierre Labouré and his worthy consort were souls of lively faith who put their trust in divine Providence and heeded little the suggestions of worldly prudence.

Catherine Labouré, their ninth child, was born on Friday, May 2, 1806. The following day, May 3, Feast of the Invention of the Holy Cross, the favored child was baptized by the Rev. Father George Mamer, pastor of the parish and formerly a Benedictine of Moutiers. The baptismal register of

7

the parish as well as that of the mayoralty, record
the name of Catherine only, although she was
familiarly called Zoé probably in honor of the saint
whose feast is kept on the second of May. While
both at home and in the village the young girl will
bear the name of Zoé, she does not waive her right
when there is question of an official act as we see
on the occasion of the baptism of a little one for
whom at twenty she stood sponsor and to whom
she gave her own name Catherine Zoé. She signs
the register Catherine Labouré, Zoé.

Catherine Zoé! These two names, the first given
at baptism, the second bestowed by family affection,
seem to symbolize the pure life of our Blessed
Sister. But to whom after God and Our Lady did
she owe the innocence of her childhood, the preservation of her virtue and her virginity if not to her
mother? It has been remarked that "to an illustrious son is ever given a wonderful mother," and as
the history of the saints often examples this law
of maternal influence, we may easily understand the
power Madeleine Gontard, that noble type of a
Christian mother, exerted over her favored child.

FAIN-LES-MOUTIERS

At the age of nine, just as she had begun to appreciate her mother's care, our little Zoé was deprived of this support. On October 9, 1815, the worthy wife of Pierre Labouré, the devoted mother of eleven children, gave up her soul to God. May it not be that in the school of sanctity, suffering next to the training of a good mother has greatest educative value? The heart of the child now turned instinctively to her heavenly Mother. It was about this time that she was one day surprised by a servant who discovered her perched on a table, her little arms embracing a statue of the Virgin.

But to what earthly guidance would Pierre Labouré entrust Zoé and Tonine during the formative period? The good father appreciated full well that a more sympathetic atmosphere must be provided than that of a home made desolate by sad bereavement and by the departure of his sons who in turn left the paternal roof for individual interests. He was not the one to imagine that his eldest daughter Marie Louise, the companion of his hearth and the guardian of little Augustus, could bestow on them the affection their souls craved. It was then to his

9

sister Marguerite who had married Antoine Jeanrot
and who was at the time the mother of four children, that the fond father confided his little treasures. Their home in the village of Saint Remy,
near the castle of that name, at one time in the
possession of the uncles of Saint Bernard was situated between Montbard and Fain-les-Moutiers.

"For two years she remained with us," says
Claudine, "my cousin Catherine by her saintly life
edified us constantly," a statement corroborated by
Father Lalourcey, pastor of the parish. But their
sojourn with their aunt was soon to terminate.
Engrossed by business cares which precluded her
personal attention to the children, Madame Jeanrot
resorted to the services of a maid. Pierre Labouré,
moreover, deprived of his eldest daughter whom
God had called to a higher life and who was at the
time in the novitiate of the Daughters of Charity in
Paris, looked to his Zoé and Tonine to fill the void
thus created. To Zoé endowed with an intellect
far beyond her twelve years, her father's resolve
was the occasion of ineffable joy. When telling
the good tidings to her little sister she gleefully

exclaimed: "Now we will together manage the house." In this generous disposition she withdrew from Saint Remy.

It was shortly after her return to Fain that she received her First Holy Communion. Striking co-incidence this, that the church of Moutiers where this future Daughter of Saint Vincent tasted for the first time of the celestial banquet, should select as its patronal feast, January twenty-fifth, the date of the establishment of the Congregation of the Mission by Saint Vincent de Paul, a choice which doubtless had its origin in the tender affection of Father Chandenier, the Abbot of Moutiers, for the apostle of charity.

We have no reason to think that Zoé Labouré was acquainted with these historic memories. But who will refuse to believe that the future Daughter of Saint Vincent attracted the loving glance of him whom she will one day delight to call her Blessed Father? Certain it is on that eventful day the seeds of a vocation began to sink in the soil of the pure heart of her who at the tender age of twelve years edified her companions by her angelic fervor.

BLESSED CATHERINE LABOURÉ

It is Tonine who to convey the spiritual attainment of her sister Catherine calls her a "mystic," a mystic as interpreted by the early biographers of Saint Bernard who describe the great reformer as one devoted to meditation *"mire cogitativus."* "Indeed," continues Antoinette, "from her earliest childhood but more especially from the epoch of her First Holy Communion Zoé cherished a filial devotion to the Blessed Virgin."

The life of our Blessed Sister at Fain-les-Moutiers may be epitomized in three words which embrace all that is essential in a profoundly spiritual life, namely, labor, penance and prayer. At first with the aid of a woman servant, later assisted by Antoinette alone, Catherine applied to the labors of the house with unremitting assiduity. The work of the kitchen, the meals for the farmhands, the supervision of the house, each was managed with equal concern. And the delicate little Augustus, what loving tenderness was lavished on the child! According to the testimony of her brothers, all that Catherine did was well and quickly done, and her father, though naturally severe, rarely found an occasion to reproach her for neglect of duty. Even among the villagers Catherine and her sister Antoinette were recognized as model housekeepers.

But what constituted Zoé's favorite diversion was the care of the pigeon house. Her appearance was the signal for hundreds of her pets to gather round her, encircling her head as if to crown her with an aureola symbolic of her innocence and simplicity.

Industry unaccompanied by prayer and penance appeared of little worth to this devoted child. To her excessive labors therefore she added practices of austere piety, fasting always on Friday and Saturday. It occurred to Tonine, the sole confidante of her pious practice, that Catherine should mitigate her eagerness for penance and with a view to this she threatened to warn her father.

"Very well, do so" at once replied Catherine curtly and in a tone indicative of a temperament little inclined to condescension.

The discreet father being apprised, contented himself with some slight observations and for the rest left this child of predilection to follow her attraction to a life of penance sustained by the spirit of prayer which became the food of her soul.

During her leisure moments Catherine took delight in repairing to the church of Fain which adjoined the Labouré farm. Near the entrance may still be seen a Burgundian statue of the Mother Most Admirable, the Infant in her lap bearing a bunch of grapes in His tiny hand. Touching scene which recalls the wish so ingenuously expressed by Sister Catherine in her last illness that it would gratify her to taste once more the fruit of the home of her childhood.

On entering the church one perceives on the whitened walls of the nave the Stations of the Cross, the gift either of Catherine or of her eldest sister. On the epistle side hangs a picture ever fondly cherished by Sister Catherine, representing the Immaculate with arms extended and feet crushing the head of the serpent, an attitude recognized as early as the eighteenth century. In a slight recess near the sanctuary is the Labouré Chapel, formerly known as the Chapel of the Holy Souls, owing to a foundation of Masses for the deceased,

14

the conditions of which are engraved on a memorial tablet in seventeenth century characters.

The Chapel of the Virgin originally separated from the body of the church was the rendezvous whither our Sister withdrew to satisfy the longings of her soul. Here it was that kneeling long hours on the pavement in the silence of prayer she contracted arthritis of the knees, to relieve which she refused even in her old age to consent to the use of a cushion.

Just as the student Bernard while offering his prayer at the altar of the Virgin in the Church of Saint Vorles, imbibed that ardent devotion to the Mother of God which merited for him the appellation of inspired songster of Mary, *"eitharista Mariae,"* so the glowing fervor which ravished the youthful heart of Catherine Labouré as she knelt in prayer before the Virgin of Fain was a fitting prelude to the favors which will win for her the title of "Seer of Rue du Bac."

But the church of Fain-les-Moutiers failed to satisfy the spiritual craving of this angelic soul who in 1844 will write thus to her sister: "You have, I dare say, forgotten the religious character of that part of the country: only one Mass on Sunday and to secure this the pastor of a neighboring parish must duplicate. Vespers are sung by the school-master; no Benediction, and as for confession, well, one must go in search of the confessor. Judge for yourself whether in such a dearth of spirituals one can feel content. For my part, under such conditions I am convinced that it is impossible to give oneself to God."

How were these difficulties which existed in the girlhood of our Sister even in a more marked degree, surmounted? In answer to this query we have the statement of a Daughter of Charity of the asylum near Moutiers-Saint-Jean: "As often as possible the Servant of God attended daily Mass in our chapel." And with what fervor she prayed! "There" said one who had times without number observed her, "is the spot where she knelt, her attitude that of an angel."

From the pastor of Sens who in turn is indebted to one of his oldest parishioners, we have the following: "Mark in what veneration Catherine La-

bouré was held even by children of her own age.
On the occasions of the parish festival of Cormarin
her presence was always a source of pleasure to all.
How gentle and amiable! Ever condescending
toward her companions. Did any contention arise
Catherine became the little peacemaker. Even at
this early period charity filled her heart for at the
sight of the needy she gladly dispensed the dainties
she might have legitimately enjoyed."

"And her presence at Mass" continues the nar-
rator, "was a veritable invitation to prayer. Assuredly it was a little saint whom the Queen of
Heaven was preparing......."

Well and truly did the good old woman testify.
And in recalling the blessings with which God
gifted her, this humble child of Fain-les-Moutiers
could, as did her heavenly Mother, intone a Magnificat of gratitude and love. Verily could she ex-
claim: "Thou O God hast singularly blessed me!
Few are they who preserve such pure and sweet
memories of early childhood! On whatsoever side
I turn I must acknowledge Thy protecting Hand.

17

BLESSED CATHERINE LABOURÉ

To Thee I offer my hymn of grateful thanksgiving
for Thou hast kept me from misfortunes which
overwhelm the soul with anguish well-nigh incon-
solable.''

CHAPTER II

HER VOCATION

1824—1830

TO belong to God was the prevailing ambition of the early years of Catherine Labouré. But from the epoch of her First Holy Communion her only aspiration was to become a consecrated spouse of Christ. Many a time did Zoé, her body weary with labor but her spirit lifted above the things of earth, discourse with her sister Antoinette about her vocation. How she sighed for that day when Tonine's strength would permit her to assume the responsibilities of the household! The still, silent voice that invited her to a higher life thrilled her soul with that pure joy that is born of heaven.

But to what community was she to direct her

steps? In her perplexity a solution is offered the young girl in what she speaks of in her old age as a dream. She was praying in her favorite chapel in the church of Fain. At the altar a venerable priest was offering the Holy Sacrifice. The Mass over, the celebrant, as if wishing to speak with her, beckoned her to approach. The child affrighted withdrew but the penetrating glance of the venerable old priest pursued her. On leaving the church Zoé visited a sick person. Again her eyes met the same kindly face but this time she heard distinctly the prophetic words: "My child, you do well to nurse the sick. You flee from me now, but one day you will be happy to come to me. The good God has His designs on you. Do not forget." Then the vision vanished. But was it a dream? Who was the priest and what did he mean?

At Moutiers-Saint-Jean the Daughters of Charity conducted a small hospital well known to Zoé Labouré. The institution dates from the seventeenth century, from the very time of Saint Vincent de Paul and owes its existence to the liberality of Claude Charles de Rochechouart de Chandenier,

HER VOCATION

Abbot and Commander of the Royal Abbey of Moutiers.

There is nothing more touching than the holy friendship between the former little shepherd of Landes and the noble house of the Abbots of Chandenier. "I know not" said Vincent de Paul, speaking of Louis Chandenier, Abbot of Tournus, "what attracted that nobleman into our miserable Company or what induced him to desire so ardently to present himself to God clothed in the poor habit of the Congregation of the Mission."

"Alas!" added the holy Founder, "only the heavenly home of our Company deserved to receive him in quality of missionary; our earthly abode, without meriting it, has been enriched by the precious inheritance of the example of his saintly life."

It was Claude, Abbé of Moutiers-Saint-Jean, who bequeathed to Vincent, whom he honored as his father, a heritage no less highly esteemed, the erection of the Confraternity of Charity. From the records of the hospital we read that he secured the services of two Daughters of Charity for the succor of the poor sick of Moutiers and the environs.

But this did not suffice his zeal. Desiring to promote not only the spiritual but also the temporal welfare of his people, the good Abbé was inspired to establish a hospital known as Saint-Sauveur. Tradition relates that Father Chandenier entreated his esteemed friend Vincent de Paul to select the site for the hospital and that it was on the occasion of this visit to Moutiers that the Abbé had a portrait of the holy priest taken. This picture together with other objects used by their Blessed Father during his sojourn, became on the death of the Reverend Abbé, the property of the Sisters of the hospital. It cannot be doubted that Zoé Labouré had often seen this portrait to which the Sisters gave a prominent place in their chapel. But it is certain likewise that she viewed it with apparently little attention since she failed to recall it on seeing the venerable priest of her dream.

In 1830 Sister Catherine Soucial was Sister Servant or Superior of the Hospital of Saint-Sauveur. A native of Landes, she followed the call that came to her as she knelt before the altar of Our Lady of Buglose, and repaired to Rue du Bac, Paris. After her novitiate she was stationed at Châtillon-sur-Seine whence in 1793 the violence of the Revolution forced the Sisters to withdraw. Her first thought was to return to her parental home but on learning that the hospital at Moutiers-Saint-Jean was as yet undisturbed, she betook herself thither. And so what promised to be but a provisional home, became for her the abode of sixty long years.

When Catherine Labouré first visited the hospital, Sister Soucial had spent well-nigh thirty years in the place. True to the teachings of Saint Vincent and versed in the experimental knowledge of the ways of Providence, the good Superioress was far from inducing the Daughter of Pierre Labouré to enter among the religious family of which she was a member. Zoé probably considering herself too young, evinced no disposition to speak of her vocation.

Notwithstanding her reticence, she was resolute in her resistance to whatever might conflict with her abiding attraction for the religious life. Many desirable offers of marriage were made her but

23

she was instant in her refusal, saying sweetly that long ago she was affianced to Jesus, her loving Savior, and would have no other. More and more intense waxed her ardor to follow the divine call. She believed the time had come to disclose to her beloved father her longing desire to take the blessed path trodden years before by her sister Marie Louise. She thought to comfort him by representing Antoinette, now about twenty years of age, as a most devoted daughter in whose hands his interests would not suffer.

But Pierre Labouré positively refused his consent. Quite sufficient, he argued, to have lost to the family of Saint Vincent, his eldest daughter. The sacrifice of his favorite, Catherine, he deemed superior to his strength and certainly contrary to his best interests. It is possible that he recalled his one time dream of embracing Holy Orders and his indecision, and perhaps meant to test his daughter's vocation. Be that as it may, he determined to expose his cherished child to the distractions of the great city of Paris. With this intent he resolved to place her in the home of her brother

24

HER VOCATION

Charles Labouré who conducted there a small restaurant for working-men, enjoining on his son the obligation of dissuading her from so illusory a project.

Wearied and depressed by all these artifices, Zoé was still steadfast in her resolution. In her anxiety she sought the advice and encouragement of her sister, Superioress of one of the houses of the Daughters of Charity in the south of France. Sister M. Louise was not slow to respond. Her letter, breathing the highest esteem and tenderest love for her holy calling, describes with exactitude the life, spirit and vocation of a Daughter of Saint Vincent. We insert it in its entirety:

Castelsarrasin, 1829

My beloved Zoé:

The grace of our Lord be forever with us!

I am at a loss how to express the gratitude I experienced on reading your dear letter. I have too great an affection for you not to be moved at the sentiments of love and esteem with which God has inspired you for a vocation so dear to me.

25

BLESSED CATHERINE LABOURÉ

You tell me that you long for this happiness. Oh! could you but know its excellence! Should God speak to your heart and make known to you His holy will, let nothing prevent you from giving yourself to the service of so good a Master. This grace I earnestly ask for you. Endeavor to render yourself worthy of this favor by loving the good God who has delivered us from the power of the devil, redeemed us by the shedding of His Precious Blood and promised to reward all we do for Him by a hundredfold in this life, and in the next, by a share in His eternal kingdom.

God forbid that I should esteem these promises of the Savior applicable to religious souls only. They are for all who aspire to perfection which, after all, is but the accomplishment of the precept of the love of God and the neighbor.

To return to the subject of our vocation. Would that I might give you even a slight idea of its advantages! What is it to be a Daughter of Charity? It is to give oneself without reserve to God for the service of His poor, His suffering members, to console the unfortunate, to be the spiritual mothers

26

of innocent children whom unnatural parents have abandoned, to care for the afflicted, to visit the sick and to prepare the dying to meet a merciful Savior.

What a calling! Nothing less than to imitate the life of Jesus Christ who went about doing good. Is it not to be, as it were, messengers of His mercy, dispensers of His charity, showing forth His divine attractions, drawing from His Sacred Heart sentiments of devotedness and love especially in favor of the little children with whom He charges us, as His apostles of charity?

The religious state is apparently more perfect than ours, and the contemplative more closely united to God. Like the mystical dove she moans in secret, and with uplifted hands implores the divine mercy. Now the Daughter of Charity surpasses her in the sublimity of her functions and in the splendor of her victories, and like the cloistered nun she must possess the same purity of heart and body, the same detachment from creatures. A religious may be compared to a soldier who in time of peace guards the city; a Daughter of Charity to one who faces the enemy. Both are entitled to the

27

gratitude of the nation, but he who combats will receive the greater honor, his courage and fidelity having been more severely tried.

True we are not called to the austere practices of the cloister, the haircloth, the discipline, etc. These we replace by our works which in the eyes of the world, because it does not comprehend the reward and the interior consolation attending self-sacrifice, appear very painful indeed. These consolations are so stupendous that had one the power and inclination to offer me, I will not say a kingdom, but the whole world, I should regard it as the mere dust at my feet, so convinced am I that the possession of the entire world would not compensate me for the happiness I experience in my vocation.

It is not customary for us to influence subjects to enter our Community I trust our good God will pardon my weakness in your regard. He knows that the salvation of your soul is as dear to me as my own, and how ardently I desire you to be numbered among those to whom it will be said: "I was hungry and you gave me to eat, thirsty and you gave me to drink, sick and you ministered unto me, naked and you clothed me, a prisoner and you visited me." Behold the life work of a true Daughter of Charity!

Consider whether during the short time allotted to us in this life, a few hours perhaps, it is not better to serve God than the world. How sweet the reward God gives to His servants, but the votaries of the world, how bitter their portion! Daily experience is my witness. Should, then, God call you, prefer Him to all else. You owe all to Him. If after recognizing in yourself a vocation to our Company, you experience some repugnance in the thought that you will not be with me, be generous and make the sacrifice to God. His Providence will in His own good time effect our meeting. Let this be our resolution, to abandon ourselves to His care. So far as lies in my power, I shall do what depends on me for your welfare.

I think it wise to accept the invitation to spend some time with our dear sister-in-law, since you will find there opportunities for improving yourself. Education is always an asset. Endeavor to acquire a better knowledge of French; you might also apply yourself to reading and arithmetic, but above all to piety and the love of the poor.

Sister M. Louise Labouré

U. D. O. C. S. O. t. S. P.

This sister-in-law, Mlle. Jane Gontard, had married her cousin, Hubert, eldest brother of Catherine Labouré, and resided at Châtillon-sur-Seine. Her husband had a splendid career. Having enlisted as a volunteer under the first Empire, he was decorated with the medal of Saint Helena, served as Body Guard under Charles X, became Lieutenant, afterwards Captain of the Gendarmery and Knight of the Legion of Honor. He died in 1865 regretted by all who knew him.

In 1829 Madame Hubert Labouré directed at Châtillon a boarding school patronized by the nobility of the environs. The house, originally a Carmelite convent, was converted by Madame Labouré into a private residence, No. 24 Rue Bourg-à-Mont. Under the name of the Institution Jeanne d'Arc, the Labouré School was removed to its present location, No. 3 Rue des Avocats.

HER VOCATION

To this school with the ready consent of her father whose chief feeling was one of relief and conviction that his daughter would alter her resolution, came the little aspirant to the religious life. Ill at ease among young ladies whose tastes, more or less frivolous, were a decided contrast to her simple manners, Zoé made no great progress. Ever and anon an irresistable attraction impelled her toward a humble dwelling situated on the right bank of the Seine, in that portion of the city termed the "Jews' Quarter," Rue de la Haute Juiverie.

Of this abode which was captivating the heart of the child, albeit she was plunged in an atmosphere of aristocracy and worldliness, writes the Abbé Frérot, Dean of Châtillon and later Bishop of Angoulème: "If you follow this street of Vieux-Bourg well known to the unfortunate, you will arrive at a house of unpretentious appearance, standing within a small court surrounded by an iron railing cast in the ornate style of Louis XV. A statue of Saint Vincent de Paul sheltering two waifs beneath his mantle indicates that you are on the threshold of an asylum where helplessness and misery ever find sympathy and protection. Pause for a few moments and you will behold the flutter of the cornette of the Daughter of Charity as she comes and goes, now ministering to the needs of the poor of the city, again distributing food to the hungry passerby or giving remedies to some child for a sick parent, greeting each with a kind and encouraging word. It is the Dispersary of Mercy, formerly known as the House of Charity."

The first time Zoé Labouré entered the House of Charity, she was struck with alarm at a picture that hung in the parlor.

"The very priest I saw in my dream," she said instinctively, designating the portrait.

"My child," replied Rev. Vincent Henry Prost, Pastor of Châtillon, who had been apprised of the event, "my child, I believe the old man who appeared in your dream was Saint Vincent de Paul who is calling you to be a Daughter of Charity."

In 1828 the administration of the house at Châtillon devolved on Sister Josephine Cany. The new

32

HER VOCATION

Superioress was ably assisted in her ministrations
of charity by a chosen soul, Sister Frances Victoria
Séjole. Sister Victoria's initiation at Châtillon was
fraught with difficulties. The young girls of the
workroom, recently established in the house and
assigned to our Sister, were insubordinate to the
extent that one of them boasted that she would
obey only when she had seen Sister Victoria stitch
the cuff of a garment as perfectly as she herself
could do it. Despite her inexperience, the young
Sister triumphed by her virtue, and the unruly
pupils yielded to her influence, a complete transfor-
mation was effected in them.

In 1829 the important duty of visiting the sick
in their homes, was confided to Sister Victoria. It
was probably on these errands of charity that she
became acquainted with the Servant of God, and
learned to appreciate her rare virtue. Aware of
her holy aspirations, she entreated her Superioress
to admit as a postulant the humble child of Fain-
les-Moutiers, saying: "Receive Zoé Labouré. Hers
is a vocation after the heart of Saint Vincent."
And the former schoolmistress proffered to con-

33

tinue during her postulatum the instruction begun at boarding school.

But how obtain the consent of Pierre Labouré? This delicate mission, undertaken by Madame Hubert Labouré, met with the most unexpected success. The devoted father yielded and resigned himself to the separation from his cherished daughter, but refused however to furnish the required dowry, and once more is Zoé indebted to her generous sister-in-law.

Early in January 1830 she obtained her heart's desire—she began her postulatum with the Sisters of Châtillon-sur-Seine. The postulatum is the time of probation preluding the novitiate or period of definite trial. Among the Daughters of Charity it is of about three months' duration.

Not long after her arrival at the House of Châtillon, Catherine Labouré received from her sister the following lines which must have greatly encouraged her in her new sphere:

HER VOCATION

My beloved Sister Zoé:

The grace of our Lord be forever with us!

Your letters gave me great pleasure. I am thoroughly satisfied with the good dispositions you manifest. Your last was especially edifying.

Continue, my beloved child, to put all your trust in God, and I assure you that you will always be happy. He is a tender Father who knows well how to reward sacrifices made for His love. Surely nothing can be wanting to those who have a Father so good and so powerful. What have we to do with the goods of this world, with its joys and its fair promises? Let our one care be to appreciate the graces He vouchsafes us and to profit by them. By acting thus, we shall make Heaven sure.

Let us rise superior to trials and tribulations, to joy or sorrow, to honor or contempt, to health or sickness. Let our sole ambition be to reach the end for which we are destined. Let us serve God

35

well. Let us give Him our love. It is only by loving Him that we can here below partake of the happiness of His elect and thus enjoy a foretaste of the bliss that awaits us in our heavenly country.

The good Sister who supposes she knows me, is mistaken. I entered the Seminary June 25, 1818, where I remained seven months. Thence I came to this place where, if such be the will of my Superiors, I hope to live and die.

Sister M. Louise Labouré

U. D. O. C. S. O. t. S. P.

The postulant of Châtillon treasured these wise counsels, humbly applying herself to the performance of her daily duty. An aged servant named Mariette remarked the untiring fidelity of the Servant of God to a community exercise prescribed by the Rule which read thus: "At three o'clock they shall go on their knees and a Sister shall say aloud: '*Christus factus est pro nobis obediens usque ad mortem*, etc.,' and all shall together adore the Son of God dying for the salvation of souls and offer Him to the Eternal Father at the moment

36

when He gave up the ghost, begging Him to apply the merit of His death especially to the agonizing, to poor sinners and to the souls detained in Purgatory. Having made this act for the space of three Paters, and Aves, they shall kiss the floor and rise immediately." Says the old woman servant: "Catherine Labouré, on duty in the workroom, would repair punctually at thee o'clock to the chapel to make this act of adoration."

Faithful to her promise Sister Victoria proceeded to instruct her young charge in the principles of reading and writing as well as in the community prayers and customs. On this subject the Rule reads as follows: "Those who have permission to learn to write may so employ a half hour, at most, of the afternoon, when the Superioress or Sister Servant judges proper and when they are entirely free from all necessary occupation. Each one shall apply to this exercise in such a manner that she may be disposed to interrupt or omit it altogether when the same Superioress or Sister Servant thinks it should give place to another occupation of stricter obligation, in order that it may in no way prove

37

prejudicial to the service of the poor or to any duty of their Company." Such was the line of conduct observed by Sister Victoria toward our Blessed Sister.

From this happy and holy intercourse there resulted between these two chosen souls, a mutual affection, respect and veneration. Early in 1877, shortly before leaving this world to receive the reward of her long labors in the Master's Vineyard, Sister Victoria learned of the death of Catherine Labouré. Though ill at the time and subject to continuous drowsiness, when a Sister approaching her said:

"Good Mother Victoria, Sister Labouré has gone to God."

"Zoé is dead!" she exclaimed and the mere name of the Servant of God seemed to revive her.

When in 1830 the extraordinary favor of the apparitions in the Chapel of Rue du Bac, in Paris, was noised abroad in the Community, Sister Victoria remarked: "If the Blessed Virgin has manifested herself to a Sister of the Seminary, it must

THE SEMINARY, RUE DU BAC

be to Sister Labouré. That child is destined to receive great favors from Heaven." Her conviction on this point was so strong, that in 1842, appointed Superioress of the Hospital of Moutiers-Saint-Jean, this "good Mother Victoria" on her way to Paris for the annual retreat, was pleased to go to the House of Enghien to see Sister Catherine. She endeavored moreover to procure the same privilege for her companions, sending them in turn to visit the Blessed Servant of God, saying:

"Dear Sisters, I shall be among the dead when the name of Sister Catherine will be a 'wonder-word.' But you who shall be alive, will esteem it a great privilege to have known and conversed with this favored child of the Blessed Virgin."

It was toward the end of April 1830. The day was not far distant when Heaven would confer extraordinary favors on the daughter of Pierre Labouré. Wholly unconscious of the designs of Providence, the Servant of God, having arrived at the term of her postulatum, repaired joyfully to the Seminary of Rue du Bac.

CHAPTER III

FIRST APPARITIONS

APRIL—JULY 1830

"MY Father," wrote Sister Catherine Labouré in 1856, "you desire me to send you the de-details of the events that transpired twenty-six years ago. I consider myself incapable of the task yet I shall in all simplicity endeavor to comply with your request. I supplicate Mary, my good Mother, to recall to my mind all the various circumstances. O Mary, may it be to your greater glory and that of your dear Son!"

The Servant of God then commits to writing a history of the first apparitions which occurred between April and July 1830. Her letter addressed to Father Aladel, Priest of the Congregation of the Mission and her confessor during her seminary, will be our invariable guide in the narrative. Our part will consist in offering an explanation or in completing a statement for the sake of greater clearness.

40

FIRST APPARITIONS

Referring to her advent to the Seminary she writes: "I arrived April 21, 1830, the Wednesday before the Translation of the Relics of Saint Vincent de Paul. So happy and contented did I feel in assisting at this great celebration that it seemed to me nothing on earth held any attraction for me." The present day reader can with difficulty conceive the joy of the young Sister on the occasion to which she alludes.

On Sunday, April 25, 1830, the body of Saint Vincent which for many years had been withdrawn from public veneration, owing to the profanations of the Revolution, was restored to the piety of the faithful. Since 1815 the precious relics of the saint, justly styled "the Saint of France," lay concealed at the Mother House of the Daughters of Charity. At length the hour had sounded when these relics should receive the homage due them. In the midst of a large concourse of bishops, priests and people, they were triumphantly borne from the metropolitan church of Notre Dame to the Mother House of the Priests of the Mission, No. 95 Rue de Sèvres. The line of route was thronged with an enthusiastic populace. Windows, balconies, even the very roofs were filled with spectators eager to salute the mortal remains of the hero of charity. The ceremony over, the illustrious Archbishop of Paris, Monseigneur de Quélen, exclaimed: "How happy I am and what consolation I have this day experienced! Now the good God may send me what trials He pleases for I feel within me the strength to meet them. My heart is ready!"

Similar sentiments must have thrilled the heart of Sister Catherine on that day and during the Novena of Thanksgiving which followed. She continues: "I asked Saint Vincent for all the graces necessary for myself, for his two families and for all France. It seemed to me that the whole country stood in great need. I prayed Saint Vincent to teach me for what I ought to ask and then the grace to ask with a lively faith.

"Each day on my return from Saint Lazare whither the Sisters repaired to assist at the solemn novena, I experienced an unutterable sadness, on beholding the heart of Saint Vincent."

But where did the Servant of God discern the

heart of the Saint? Let her tell us: "I had the consolation of beholding it in our chapel, above the little shrine in which his relics are exposed." In front of the door of the sacristy, under the picture of Saint Ann, a table had been placed upon which rested the shrine mentioned by Sister Catherine. This was the scene of the apparition.

Under what form was the heart of Saint Vincent revealed? Again the Seer herself will reply: "It appeared to me on three successive days each time different from the former. The first aspect was of a pale, flesh color which denoted peace, calm, innocence and union. Next I viewed it all aflame symbolic of the charity which was to be enkindled in hearts. It seemed to me that the whole Community would be regenerated and would extend to the extremities of the earth. The third time it was of a livid hue at which my soul was overwhelmed with a sadness that I could with difficulty banish. Why or how I know not, but the sadness seemed to portend a change of government."

Is it not passing strange that this humble child with no knowledge of political affairs should be preoccupied with such a subject as a revolution? And even had she been in touch with the policy of the kingdom, how could she have conceived in a time of absolute peace, of consummate glory, its downfall? Who could foresee in latter April 1830, the disastrous events of the coming July: the bloodshed and the fall of Charles X?

Let us resume the Sister's narrative: "An interior voice made known to me: 'The heart of Saint Vincent is greatly afflicted because of the woes about to fall on France.'" On the last day of the octave she saw the same heart vermilion in color and the interior voice whispered: "The heart of Saint Vincent is somewhat consoled since he has obtained through Mary's intercession that his two families shall not perish amid these disasters and that God will make use of them to revive faith."

She then concludes the account of the first apparition by the expression of her entire submission: "I could not refrain from speaking of the occurrence to my confessor who relieved my anxiety by admonishing me to think no more about it, and to give myself no further inquietude."

44

FIRST APPARITIONS

This confessor is none other than the Rev. Father Aladel to whom the present letter is addressed. Prudently indeed did this priest, scarcely thirty years of age, act in counseling the Servant of God "to think no more about it," direction justified by his age and inexperience as well as by the character of the communication of his penitent. He apparently attached but little importance to this first revelation.

On her part Sister Catherine retired into the silence of the Seminary. Her only ambition was to pass unnoticed among her companions. No one either in the Seminary or elsewhere, except Father Aladel, had the remotest idea of the remarkable favors granted our Blessed Sister, nor did anyone suspect what a treasure Heaven had confided to the family of Saint Vincent.

In proof of this assertion we quote the following letter from the Superioress of Castelsarrasin, Sister M. Louise Labouré, dated May 1830:

BLESSED CATHERINE LABOURÉ

My beloved Zoé:

The grace of our Lord be forever with us!

I have just learned with great pleasure that you are now at the Community. Your silence since the twenty-fourth of March has made me anxious, for I feared you might have changed your mind. I greatly pitied you. However the good dispositions manifested in your last letter somewhat reassured me.

Now I am satisfied. I no longer pity you. I give thanks to God and supplicate Him to grant you the spirit of our holy state and perseverance therein, a favor which He never refuses to those who correspond to His grace.

Upon receiving my letter unless you have something special to communicate wait a while before writing. I am soon to send a postulant to the Seminary though the exact day of her departure is not yet decided. She will deliver my messages to you verbally should I fail to find time to write. When you become better acquainted with your surroundings you may write me. I have no anx-

46

iety for your future. Your happiness is as great as can be expected on earth, and its increase will be in proportion to the docility with which you comply with the good counsels which shall never be wanting to you.

It is to be hoped that you left your self-will on the road from Châtillon to Paris. If so, I congratulate you. Do not seek to reclaim it. The decisions of Superiors in our regard are better far than our own. Bear in mind that you are no longer in your own home, and be persuaded that you are incapable of doing anything. In this conviction you will assuredly attain the desired goal.

During your Seminary, my dear one, endeavor to acquire a store of virtue, especially of humility. A little reflection should convince one that there is no difficulty in esteeming oneself the last of all in the house of the Lord where all places are honorable. Indeed the last place should be preferred. I greatly desire that you may understand this truth and reduce it to practice.

I believe you are now in retreat. Love God and pray for me. Assure our worthy Mothers of the

47

Seminary, especially our beloved Mother Martha,
of my respectful and affectionate remembrance.
With what great pleasure we recall her holy in-
structions! I am sending her a letter by our
postulant who will probably leave us the early
part of next week.

Meanwhile pray for me and believe me always
in the love of Jesus and Mary,

Your devoted Sister

M. Louise Labouré

U. D. O. C.

Mother Martha, mentioned in the above letter,
was at that time the Directress of the Seminary.
The term Mother, then in use, admirably suited the
kind and saintly woman who for so many years
edified the Community of Rue du Bac and trained
numerous Daughters of Charity for the service of
the poor. Of the intercourse between this worthy
Mother and Sister Catherine, we know nothing. It
is alleged however, that Sister Ann Cailhot, Third
Directress of the Seminary, a soul whose patience
throughout a most painful malady amounted to
heroism, on one occasion peremptorily called the

48

young Sister to order in the refectory, thus ad-
dressing her:

"Well, Sister Labouré, are you still in ecstasy?"

The fact is the favored Seer ravished by the
beauty of the vision she had just contemplated in
the chapel, was oblivious to the meal served her.
That these apparitions rapidly succeeded one another, we glean from the account of 1856. The
narrative of the Sister runs thus:

"I was moreover favored by another great grace,
that of the visible presence of our Lord in the
Adorable Sacrament. This happiness was mine
throughout the whole course of my seminary,
except when I doubted. Then, fearing I was
deceived and wishing to penetrate the mystery, I
saw nothing."

What a charming simplicity and perfect humility
are revealed by this acknowledgment! It is hardly
necessary to add that the doubt expressed by the
Servant of God does not refer to the mystery of the
Real Presence of Jesus in the Blessed Sacrament,
the object of our Catholic Faith, but merely the

49

reality of the extraordinary vision of which she deemed herself unworthy.

The great privilege accorded to Sister Catherine during the period of her seminary assumed a new character on Sunday, June 6, 1830.

"On Trinity Sunday during Mass our Lord appeared to me in the Most Holy Sacrament as a king. He wore on His breast a cross. At the gospel, I saw the cross and all the regal ornaments fall at His feet, our Lord remaining thus despoiled. Upon this my mind was a prey to sad and gloomy thoughts for I understood that the king would be deprived of his royalty and that many miseries would follow."

The gloomy forebodings of the Seer were about to be realized. On the night of the eighteenth of July 1830, the Blessed Virgin will announce to Sister Catherine many sorrowful events of immediate occurrence as well as other painful happenings of a more remote period. She will moreover declare that her divine Son is about to entrust to His humble servant a mission the purport and extent of which will not be at once understood. A glorious mission withal, to which all the favors hitherto granted our Blessed Sister, converge as to a common centre. A divine mission which will determine the Manifestation of the Virgin Immaculate, November 27, 1830.

That the reader may note the ingenuous simplicity and unction of her language, we shall give the details of the preliminary apparition of the Blessed Virgin on the night of July eighteenth, in the favored one's own words.

"On the eve of the Feast of Saint Vincent our good Mother Martha gave an instruction on devotion to the saints, especially to the Blessed Virgin, which greatly increased my long-entertained desire of seeing the Holy Mother. A piece of the surplice worn by Saint Vincent had been distributed among us. Having cut my bit into two parts I swallowed one and fell asleep believing that Saint Vincent would obtain this favor for me. My last thought was 'I shall see the Blessed Virgin.'

"That night, at eleven-thirty, I heard my name called three times. Aroused from sleep I looked

51

in the direction whence the sound came. It seemed near the passage. Upon drawing my bed curtains, I beheld a child of four or five years who said to me: 'Come to the chapel. The Blessed Virgin awaits you!'

"My first thought was, 'We shall be discovered.'

"The child answered: 'Do not be uneasy. It is half past eleven; every one is asleep. Come, I am waiting for you.'

"I dressed hastily and advanced toward the child who had remained standing at the head of my bed. He followed me, or rather I followed him and wherever we passed, he always kept to my left. As we went along, to my astonishment I found all the lamps lighted, but my amazement reached its height when at the mere touch of the child's hand the door swung open and revealed the chapel ablaze with the splendor of a midnight Mass.

"But I did not see the Blessed Virgin. The child conducted me into the sanctuary, over to the chair used by the Director. Meanwhile I knelt,

FIRST APPARITIONS

the child standing. As the time of waiting seemed long, I looked anxiously toward the gallery fearing lest the Sisters on night watch might be passing. At length the desired moment came.

"The child said: 'There is the Blessed Virgin.'

"I then heard a sound proceeding from the gallery near the picture of Saint Joseph. It was like the rustling of a silk dress. I saw a lady descend the steps of the altar, on the gospel side, and seat herself in a chair similar to that represented in the picture of Saint Ann. But her countenance was unlike Saint Ann's." The Sister here alludes to the picture of the mother of the Virgin, still seen above the door of the sacristy.

"I doubted whether it was the Blessed Virgin. Then the child said: 'Behold the Blessed Virgin.' At this moment I experienced an indescribable emotion. I asked myself if I was really in the presence of the Mother of God. Suddenly the child assuming the voice of a man spoke aloud in a commanding tone. Then casting a glance at the Blessed Virgin, I sprang forward, throwing myself

53

on my knees on the steps of the altar. I rested my hands on the knees of the Blessed Virgin.

"At this instant I tasted the sweetest joy of my life, a delight beyond expression. Then it was that she told me how I was to act toward my director and revealed to me many other things which I am not at liberty to disclose. She instructed me how to bear my trials, telling me to come here indicating with her left hand, the foot of the altar, to pour out my heart. She assured me that I should receive here all the consolation necessary for me. I asked her the meaning of all these things and she graciously explained all.

"I am unable to say how long a time I remained kneeling at her side. All I know is that the Blessed Virgin withdrew by the same way she had entered, vanishing like a shadow.

· "Having arisen from the altar steps, I found the child just where I left him. He said to me 'She has gone.' We returned as we had come, the child always bearing to my left. He was clothed in white, resplendent with light and appeared to be

54

APPARITION OF JULY 18, 1830

about four or five years. I believe he was my guardian angel who rendered himself visible to conduct me to the chapel where I might see the Blessed Virgin. Indeed I had prayed earnestly for this favor. Having returned to my bed I heard the clock strike two. I slept no more."

Such in its simplicity, humility and precision, in a word, in its perfect truthfulness is the account of the apparition of the night of July eighteenth. And what simplicity! For some time Sister Catherine had desired "to see" the Blessed Virgin, to see her with her eyes and touch her with her hands! No ordinary boon this. It is a remarkable fact that among the favored souls of the nineteenth century Sister Catherine seems to be alone in the enjoyment of personal contact with our heavenly Mother. Did she not rest her virginal hands on the knees of the Queen of Angels?

Mark this one touch of unmistakable humility. The Sister is convinced that the child who awakened her is her guardian angel. She says of the angel: "He followed me." Then recognizing the claims of humility and truth she adds "or rather, I followed him." No detail escapes the analysis of the favored Seer. Her pen describes the least circumstances of the vision. The chair used by the Virgin is similar to that represented in the picture of Saint Ann, but the personal appearance of the Blessed Mother is strikingly different from that of the saint in the picture. Albeit the Sister lacks the power to express it, still all the beauty of that countenance is felt, and in this very inability to delineate its perfection, we discover exactitude. The child-guide calls her from the passage; awaits her at the head of the bed; remains standing but does not advance farther. Again, on their way to the chapel the child keeps to the left; remains standing during the apparition; seeks her left on returning from the chapel; seems to be about four or five years old, etc., etc. What precision of detail!

And the various impressions experienced by her during the apparition—does she not enumerate them with the rigor, if not the technicality, of a psychologist? Her fear of being heard if she rises; her astonishment on finding the chapel brilliantly illuminated; her furtive glance toward the gallery apprehensive as she is of discovery; her doubt and consequent anguish on not beholding at once the Blessed Virgin. Exactitude, humility and simplicity are all here—characteristics totally antagonistic to indications of hallucination and evident proofs of supernatural truth.

During the apparition above treated, the Blessed Virgin had spoken a long time to Sister Catherine. She had told her many things which the Servant of God was not permitted to reveal, as says the letter of 1856. Twenty years later, a short time before her death, circumstances will oblige Sister Catherine to depart from this silence. She will feel interiorly urged to speak. And so we have the happiness to possess a complete account of the ever memorable interview, written in her own hand. True, she draws upon memory for these statements. But does this not furnish another motive for admiring the unity and coherence of the account, written as it is after the lapse of forty-five years?

The eminent Cardinal Bona in his "Treatise on the Discernment of Spirits" remarks that the remembrance of the extraordinary facts occurring in the mystical life, be they words or vision, endure a long time in the memory and are perhaps never eradicated therefrom. In 1876 Sister Catherine Labouré remembers distinctly the words spoken to her by the Virgin in 1830. We give here the authentic version.

An interview with the Blessed Virgin from 11 p. m. July eighteenth to 1: 30 a. m. July nineteenth, Feast of Saint Vincent:

"My child, the good God wishes to charge you with a mission. You will suffer many trials but you will surmount them, knowing that you endure them for the glory of God. You will know what comes from the good God. You will be tormented by it until you have revealed it to him who is charged to direct you. You will be contradicted but you will have grace. Do not fear. Speak with simplicity and confidence. You will see certain things; render an account of them. You will be inspired in your meditations.

"The times are evil. Misfortunes are about to fall upon France. The throne will be overturned.

58

The whole world will be afflicted by miseries of every kind"—while she said this the Blessed Virgin appeared much grieved—"but come to the foot of this altar. Here graces will be bestowed on all who ask with confidence and fervor. They will be given to the great and to the lowly.

"My child, I especially love to bestow favors on the Community. Well do I love it. But there are some things that grieve me. There exist great abuses: the Rule is disregarded; regularity is not observed; relaxation exists in both Communities. Tell this to him who has charge of you. Although he is not the Superior he will in time be charged in an especial way with the Community. He must do all in his power to restore the exact observance of Rule. Tell him so for me. Let him be vigilant concerning the reading, loss of time, visits, etc. . . . .

"When the Rule shall be in vigor a community will seek to unite itself with yours. This is not customary. but I approve it. Tell them to receive it. God will bless the union; great peace will result and the Community will increase and extend.

59

"But there will come great misfortunes. The danger will be iminent, but do not fear. The good God and Saint Vincent will protect the Community"—the Blessed Virgin seemed very sad. "I also will be with you. I have always watched over you. I will bestow many graces upon you. The moment will come when the danger will be great; all will seem to be lost but have confidence. I will be with you. You will recognize my visit and the protection of God and Saint Vincent over both Communities.

"It will not be so with other communities. There will be victims.". . . —Tears filled the eyes of the Blessed Virgin as she said this. "There will be victims among the clergy of Paris. Monseigneur, the Archbishop, will die. My child, the cross will be despised; blood will flow in the streets"—here the emotion of the Blessed Virgin was so great that she could not speak. "My child" she continued, "the whole world will be in desolation."

"I considered when this should be: 'forty years and ten and then peace.' "

Another version of this interview concludes as

follows: "At these words I thought 'When will this take place?' I perfectly understood forty years."

On this point Father Aladel asked: "Do you know whether you or I shall witness these things?"

"I answered: 'If we do not, others will.' "

Such are the words of Catherine Labouré relative to the ineffable privilege of her interview with the Blessed Virgin, July 18, 1830.

The first and most important of these revelations is that which the Seer reproduces in exactly the same terms in her twofold recital: "My child, the good God wishes to charge you with a mission." The nature of this mission is not revealed. It is God's secret; but the fact is beyond doubt. The young Sister then receives from her heavenly Mother certain counsels for the direction of her personal conduct in the accomplishment of this mission. Simplicity and openness of heart toward the guide of her conscience are advised but above all, great confidence regardless of the obstacles she may meet.

Finally, as a pledge as it were, of the reality of her divine mission, the future is disclosed to her view. Father Aladel, Chaplain of the Mother House, will one day fill the office of Director of the Daughters of Charity. He will, moreover, labor to reform the specified abuses, offshoots of revolutionary disorder. "There will be a marvelous increase in the two families of Saint Vincent de Paul. . . ." The Community of the Sisters of Charity, founded by Mother Seton in the United States, will obtain July 7, 1849, the exceptional favor of union with the Daughters of Charity. The Congregation of Mlle. de Brandis in Austria and that of the Sisters of Verviers in Belgium will solicit the same favor. "Great evils will fall upon France." "To witness the literal accomplishment of this prophecy" writes the English author of 'L'Epopée Mariale en France au XIXe Siècle,' "we need but recall the events of 1830 to 1870. During the Commune the members of several religious communities, many of the clergy of Paris and the Archbishop, Monseigneur Darboy, suffered death,—'blood flowed in the streets.' "

FIRST APPARITIONS

The words terminating the prophecy, "forty
years, and ten, then peace".... need explanation.
Owing to an inaccurate and much to be regretted
interpretation, some were led to believe that the
predicted peace would occur in 1880, ten years
after the evils foretold. The author of a pamphlet
entitled "The Miraculous Medal of Mary Immaculate and the Hopes of the Church" favored
this view stating "in 1880 we may hope to see
peace restored to society now so disturbed." But
the event not corresponding with the prophecy
thus interpreted, brought discredit thereon. The
opinion soon spread that Sister Labouré to whom
the manifestation of the medal had been made, had
uttered some prophecies of wonderful fulfillment,
while others had not been realized. It was however emphatically asserted that such errors in no
wise prejudice the sanctity of the Servant of God,
for in the event of such revelations as bear no
relation to the sanctification of the soul and are
of no spiritual efficacy, God does not especially
intervene. The same fact is recognized in the case
of canonized saints of the early centuries. Thus

the Bollandists, Amort and Father Poulain point out many errors scientific and historic, in the revelations of Saint Hildegard, Saint Elizabeth of Schoenau, of Blessed Herman Joseph, of Saint Frances of Rome, etc.

It is the fact, however, on which the interpretation rests that makes it appear contestable. We therefore present an opinion which seems more favorable to the truth. While the Sister is preoccupied about the time when the prediction will be verified, an interior voice indicates two dates. The first of these evidently refers to 1870, forty years after 1830; the second, ten years, would seem to point to 1880, if the text is understood to mean forty years and ten years. Thus we can say that the first date 1870 opens an era of bloody disasters; the second 1880 marks the introduction of legal prosecution. The epoch of the promised peace is absolutely undetermined. Sister Catherine simply writes, "and afterward peace," followed by numerous asterisks, as if to accentuate the mysterious character of her revelations.

Whatever be the opinions of the events foretold,

FIRST APPARITIONS

great evils weighing heavily on France were about to be realized. The Seer had so understood the fact and revealed it in terms sufficiently explicit.

On July 27 1830, eight days after the first apparition of the Blessed Virgin, a terrible revolution broke out. According to the statement of an eye witness: "Then were churches profaned, crosses overturned, religious communities attacked and dispersed, priests pursued and maltreated. The Archbishop of Paris, become the object of the fury of the populace, to escape the dangers that threatened his life, was obliged to disguise himself and remain concealed. It seemed as if the evil days of 1793 had returned.

The Mother House of the Daughters of Charity as well as that of the Priests of the Mission was respected. Despite the booming of cannon and the frenzy of the populace, a retreat begun at Rue du Bac continued quietly and with perfect regularity. It is true Saint Lazare was not spared domiciliary visitation, still the revolutionists committed no depredations neither did they leave a trace of their passage.

BLESSED CATHERINE LABOURÉ

In the remarks on Sister Catherine Labouré, assembled by Father Aladel, Sister Pineau for many years sacristan of the chapel of Rue du Bac, relates the following:

"There is a circumstance that should be published as it shows how secure are those whom God keeps. It proves too the truth of Sister Catherine's assuring words, never uttered in vain.

"On a certain day" continues the Sister in her simple style "a band of those famous heroes of July, having at their head a boy of twelve or fourteen years who surpassed the whole band in the noise he made, presented themselves at Rue de Sèvres demanding the arms which they pretended had been seen carried into the house. Good Father Salhorgne, then Superior General, undisguised—he had never laid aside his cassock—went forward to meet them, He attempted to reason with the boy, assuring him that he was mistaken in the notion that arms had been brought to the house, but all in vain.

"Upon this he said: 'Well, my child, perhaps you would like to see my arms '

66

FIRST APPARITIONS

" 'O yes Sir,' said the boy, 'let us see them.'

"The priest then presented the breviary which he had with him.   The child stared at it.

" 'Now would you like to see the balls I use?' Opening the book he showed him the pictures that marked the lessons.

"Leaping for joy, the poor child cried: 'O Father, what beautiful pictures!'

" 'Would you like to have one?' asked our good Father.

" 'O yes Sir,' responded the child who went off triumphantly displaying his picture.   And the whole mob followed their young leader.' "

These unfortunate wretches returned another day, this time to drag the crucifix from the entrance of the house, but remarks Sister Pineau "the energy of Father Etienne caused them to withdraw promptly.   From this time no hostile manifestation disturbed the tranquillity of the missionaries." According to the testimony of Father Etienne the young Sister had predicted this result to her confessor.

BLESSED CATHERINE LABOURÉ

Sister Catherine had also told Father Aladel that a bishop would seek refuge at Saint Lazare, that they should not hesitate to receive him, and that he would be in security there. The director of the Seminary Sister paid but little attention to this prediction. On his return from Rue du Bac to Saint Lazare he was informed by Father Salhorgne that Monseigneur de Frayssinous, Bishop of Hermopolis and Minister of Religious Worship under Charles X, had come to ask an asylum. Fearing for his safety at Saint Lazare, the Superior had stated his apprehension to the Minister who repaired to Saint-Germaine-en-Laye. Sister Pineau to whom we are indebted for this fact states: "This revelation bears the impress of truth which makes it easily recognizable."

The declarations of Sister Catherine will not always be ignored. Meanwhile the favored Seer is content to impart faithfully the heavenly messages she received awaitng the special mission to be confided to her and following the example of Mary, the Servant of God will keep all these things meditating upon them in the secret of her heart.

CHAPTER IV

MANIFESTATION OF THE IMMACULATE VIRGIN

NOVEMBER 27, 1830

WITH the following words does Sister Catherine, on August 15, 1841, introduce her account of one of the apparitions of 1830:

"Today is the feast of the Assumption of the Most Holy Virgin. O Queen so near to God, listen favorably to my prayers. It is for thee and for thy greater glory that I entreat thee to enlighten me and to impart to me the strength and courage to act for thy glory. It seems to me that I am living over again that ever memorable day so precious to me, that Saturday, eve of the first Sunday of Advent. . . . . I was convinced that I would see again the Most Holy Virgin, see her in the perfection of her beauty, and this hope was my life."

"In the perfection of her beauty." Yes, she whom the Church styles, Mother Most Admirable, will thus reveal herself to her humble servant in response to her fervent, disinterested and persever-

ing prayer. And this ardent, candid soul will understand those mysterious words spoken by Mary
during the long interview of the first apparition:
"My child, God wills to confide to you a special
mission." The mission of Sister Catherine will be
to present to the world the Blessed Virgin, not
under any one particular aspect of her incomparable
loveliness, but in the fulness of her royal splendor,
in the very "perfection of her beauty."

The importance of the Manifestation of November 27, 1830, merits the careful examination of its
various phases. In our endeavor to sacrifice neither
method nor clearness, neither doctrine nor fulness,
in a matter of such delicacy, we have decided firstly
to recount the apparition, then to establish its objective reality, and finally to sketch the main characteristics of its symbolism.

There will be little difficulty in establishing the
fact of the apparition of November 27, 1830, if we
consider in the first place, the writings of the Seer
and secondly her oral declarations gathered by
witnesses worthy of credence. In this the most

APPARITION OF NOVEMBER 27, 1830

complete of her narratives Sister Catherine thus expresses herself:

"Jesus, Mary, Joseph!"

"On November 27, 1830, Saturday preceding the first Sunday of Advent, at half past five in the afternoon, during the profound silence that followed the reading of the meditation, I seemed to hear, coming from the tribune near the picture of Saint Joseph, a noise like the rustling of a silk gown. Looking in that direction, I saw the Blessed Virgin elevated to about the height of the picture. She was clothed in white. Her robe of silk, of auroral whiteness, was fashioned in the style termed, *à la vierge*, high neck and plain sleeves. Beneath a white veil which fell to her feet, and resting lightly on the hair was a fillet with a lace edging about an inch in width. The figure was distinctly outlined. The feet rested upon a sphere, or rather a half sphere, as only half was visible. In her hands which were raised to the height of her waist, she held a ball representing the globe. Her attitude was natural and graceful; her eyes directed heavenward. . . . . the whole figure

resplendent with beauty, such beauty as I cannot
describe. . . . .

"Suddenly her fingers were adorned with rings
set with precious stones, some more beautiful than
others, some large, others small. Rays of various
degrees of brilliancy issued from them; the larger
gems emitted more resplendent rays, the smaller,
rays of lesser intensity. So flooded with light was
the lower portion of the figure that I could no
longer see her feet.

"While I contemplated her, the Blessed Virgin
lowered her eyes and looked upon me. I then heard
a voice saying to me: 'The ball which you see
represents the entire world, especially France . . . .
and each person in particular.' I cannot now express what I then saw and felt. Oh! the beauty
and the splendor of those rays! 'These rays symbolize the graces which I shed on those who ask
for them.' Hereby I understood how agreeable
to the Blessed Virgin are the prayers addressed to
her and how liberal she is toward those who invoke
her, what precious graces she would give those

who would ask them of her and with what joy she would grant them.

"At this moment I scarcely knew where I was. All I can say is that I was immersed in supreme delight, when a panel of oval shape formed around the Blessed Virgin and on it traced in golden letters were these words: 'O Mary conceived without sin, pray for us who have recourse to thee!' Then a voice said to me: 'Have a medal struck on this model. All those who wear it will receive great graces. It should be worn around the neck; great graces will be the portion of those who wear it with confidence. . . .' All at once the picture appeared to turn and I saw the reverse of the medal. Solicitous about what should be inscribed on the reverse, I seemed one day to hear a voice saying: 'The M and the two hearts are enough.' "

The original writings from which we have quoted, thus furnish an authenticated account of the Manifestation of November 27, 1830. True, certain details have been omitted, either lost sight of by the Seer at the time of the compilation, or presumably already in possession of her director.

BLESSED CATHERINE LABOURÉ

The fact that some of these are of no little moment warrents our inserting them. And here let us recall the learned suggestion of the Carmelites of Paris in their recent translation of the works of Saint Teresa: "Mystics in their writings not infrequently present but one aspect of the question under consideration. In one place they throw light on a certain phase of the truth because the Spirit of God has vouchsafed an especial illumination concerning it. Elsewhere they will demonstrate some other feature of the same truth. Is there any contradiction involved? By no means. Let us carefully gather these rays of light, scattered here and there, forming of them a luminous sheaf to enable us to discern the thought of the mystic, if not in its entirety,—we hardly hope so great a favor—at least with sufficient completeness to secure us against a false interpretation."

In another account of the apparition Sister Catherine accentuates the following details: The Blessed Virgin was of "medium height;" her robe was "high about the neck;" the veil covering her head "fell on each side to her feet;" she

74

FIRST APPARITIONS

"wore a kind of fillet on the edge of which was lace a trifle above an inch in width." The figure was not only discernible, but "very distinct;" under her feet "a white ball" was visible; her eyes were at times "raised heavenward, again lowered." The voice that instructed Sister Catherine was heard "in the depth of her heart." And the Seer concludes: "Everything gradually faded away, leaving me so thrilled with joy and consolation that I am unable to describe. . . . ."

Later on, interrogated as to whether there was not under the feet of the Virgin some emblem other than the white globe or rather half globe, mentioned in the original text, the Servant of God replied that there was also "a serpent of greenish color, spotted with yellow." Concerning the position of the hands, the manuscript describes them elevated to a certain height supporting the globe. But on the repeated testimony of the Sister, the globe having disappeared, the arms of the Blessed Virgin were extended in the attitude rendered so popular by the "Miraculous Medal" and familiarly known ten years previous to the time of the Sister's writing. The rings "numbered three on each finger; the largest near the hand, another of medium size midway between hand and finger tip, the smallest at the end of the finger; each ring was set with gems of proportionate size."

The prayer, "O Mary conceived without sin etc.," formed a half circle, beginning on a level with the right hand, passing over the head and terminating on a level with the left hand. Finally, on the reverse of the picture the Seer beheld "the monogram of the Blessed Virgin composed of the letter M surmounted by a cross with a bar at its base; beneath the M were the hearts of Jesus and Mary, the one encircled by a crown of thorns, the other pierced with a sword." As to the twelve stars which have always figured on the reverse of the Miraculous Medal, it is morally certain that this detail had been mentioned by the Sister at the time of the apparition.

While the Manifestation of the Immaculate Virgin was renewed several times at various intervals, the circumstances relative thereto are ever the same. "She appeared to me a third time," writes Sister

FIRST APPARITIONS

Catherine, "but I do not remember the date."
The favored Seer entitles her narrative which is
almost identical with the preceding "Third Apparition of the Blessed Virgin to the same Sister."
We present it in its entirety.

"Always preoccupied with the Blessed Virgin
whom I had seen, I lived in the hope of again
enjoying the privilege. On a certain day, at five-
thirty in the afternoon, during the profound silence
that followed the reading of the meditation I
seemed to hear a noise like the rustling of a silk
gown. It came from the side of the altar. In the
rear near the tabernacle I perceived the Blessed
Virgin. She was of medium height, clothed in
white; under her feet was a white globe; her silk
robe, of auroral whiteness, was fashioned in the
style known as *à la vierge*. Over her head was a
white veil which fell on each side to her feet.
Beneath this veil and resting lightly on the hair
was a bandeau edged with lace. The whole figure
was very distinct. So beautiful was she that it is
impossible to find words to describe her loveliness.

"Her hands, raised to the waist in a graceful,

easy pose, held a globe surmounted by a small golden cross. Suddenly the fingers were adorned with rings set with precious stones of great brilliancy. The rays emanating from them on all sides, so filled the space with resplendent light that the feet of the Virgin were no longer visible. Very powerful rays issued from the large stones while those that proceeded from the small gems were correspondingly small. No words can express what I learned at the moment when the Blessed Virgin offered the globe to our Lord. . . . . nor is it possible to convey the emotions I experienced.

"As I contemplated the Blessed Virgin, a voice resounded in the depth of my heart: 'These rays are symbols of the graces which the Blessed Virgin obtains for those who ask her for them.' These words should be inscribed at the feet of the Blessed Virgin."

Sister Catherine here alludes to a statue of the Virgin about which she gives in pencil the following suggestions: "The statue should be of life size; a veil should cover the head and fall to the ground; the figure distinct; a golden ball should

78

"These rays are symbols of the graces which the
Blessed Virgin obtains for those who ask for them."

be in the hands which should be raised to the waist as if offering it to God; and the fingers should be adorned with precious stones from which rays should descend to the feet covering the entire base."

The Seer further adds: "The following inscription should be traced on the base of the pedestal" which was probably to support the statue. " 'My child, this ball represents the world, especially France, and each person in particular. Mark this well; the whole world, especially France, and each person in particular. The stones that emit no rays refer to graces for which they forget to pray.' " And the Servant of God continues: "Oh! how glorious it will be to hear: 'Mary is Queen of the world, particularly of France,' and the children shall cry out in transports of joy: 'and of each person in particular.' It will be a time of joy, peace and happiness which will last long. She shall be represented on banners that will be carried throughout the world.

Another penciled note in the same tenor refers to a picture illustrating the apparition, showing details not given on the Miraculous Medal. These lines "should be placed at the base of the picture in legible characters, that all may read: 'O Mary conceived without sin, pray for us who have recourse to thee. My child, this ball represents the whole world, especially France, and each person in particular. Mark well: the entire world, especially France, and each individual. These rays that you see are graces which I bestow on those who ask for them. The stones emitting no rays symbolize graces for which they forget to ask.' "

But neither picture nor statue will satisfy the Seer. What she desires above all is that an altar commemorative of the manifestation be erected. A heaven-born desire surely which Sister Catherine exposes to her director as she concludes the narrative of 1841.

"Now I am going to tell you that for two years past I have felt urged to ask you to erect an altar in honor of the Blessed Virgin on the spot where she appeared. Now more than ever I feel urged to tell you this and to ask of you an extra Communion, yearly, for the Community. All indulgences will be granted you. Ask, ask, all will be granted . . . . . . I believe that the good God will be glorified thereby, the Blessed Virgin honored, and all hearts reanimated with fervor. I entreat you to do this for the greater glory of God and for the increase of devotion to the Most Holy Virgin. I am firmly convinced that you will neglect nothing to effect this as speedily as possible so that all may be in readiness the Saturday preceding the first Sunday of Advent. It is to satisfy my conscience that I am so persistent in entreating this favor of you. I believe God and the Blessed Virgin require this of you . . . . . I entreat you to ask this favor of our Most Honored Father.

"I am in the Sacred Hearts of Jesus and Mary
Your devoted and obedient child
Unworthy Daughter of Charity"

No other signature follows. Neither is the name of Sister Catherine affixed to any of the papers treating of the apparitions. Our Blessed Sister wished to remain in obscurity. With but one object in view, namely, the honor of the Blessed Virgin, by fidelity to the least prescriptions of obedience and by devotedness to the interests of truth, she ever strove to promote her glory.

This question now arises and claims our immediate attention: "How evaluate critically and historically the declarations of the Seer, Sister Catherine Labouré, since it is on her testimony we have based our notes?" And then by consequence comes the question: "What is the objective reality and what the supernatural truth of the apparitions of 1830, especially that of November twenty-seventh?"

From the pen of the gifted and pious author of "A Century of the Church of France"—1800-1900—we have the following: "While we are not constrained to accept the apparitions and supernatural interventions of the Blessed Virgin, still the confidence reposed in such as it is our intention to relate, justified by the bestowal of favors both corporal and spiritual and encouraged by the liberal support of the Holy See, rightly ascribes to these manifestations an eminent place in the history of the Cult of her who at Cana asked and obtained the first miracle." In another passage Monsignor

82

FIRST APPARITIONS

Baunard distinctly observes that the first of these supernatural revelations of Mary is that of the Miraculous Medal to Sister Catherine Labouré whom he styles "a humble and saintly Daughter of Charity." Recognizing that this statement assumes as true what we are actually endeavoring to prove, let us for the nonce disregard the favorable attitude of the Church concerning the sanctity of our Blessed Sister, and present the subject under a contrary aspect, thus: "Was the Servant of God in good faith in declaring what she witnessed, and if her sincerity be proved, might she not have been the dupe of an overexcited imagination?" Doubtless here we have a consideration worthy of minutest investigation.

This twofold query meets with a triumphant response in the very life of Sister Catherine, so uniform, so tranquil. We are however prepared to produce the elements which make for the solution of so significant a question, elements obtained in great measure, from no less authentic a source than the Canonical Inquiry of 1836, a treatise on the origin and effects of the Miraculous Medal.

Let us examine, in the first place, the sincerity of Sister Catherine.

It must be admitted that the veracity of the Seer has never been seriously questioned. And why should it be? "Imagine, if you can, a young girl possessing the limited education of the peasant type, endowed with the ability of devising the scheme of the picture she affirms she beheld and delineating its every detail with that precision which permitted its use as the model for a medal! Fancy such a one formulating the invocation 'O Mary conceived without sin.' Can you conceive an innocent peasant girl capable of such temerity as to promise those who should wear the medal and recite the prayer the especial protection of Mary? Is it possible for anyone, even for an instant to entertain the idea that a young Sister of the Seminary would have the effrontery to build up such a tissue of lies and then calmly repeat them to her confessor? Assuredly such cunning and duplicity are incompatible with the evidences of the remarkable simplicity, candor and innocence of this young woman." Thus we must accept in their entirety,

84

FIRST APPARITIONS

the declarations of the Promoter of the Canonical
Inquiry instituted by His Grace, Archbishop de
Quélen, in 1836.

"What motive, moreover, could have prompted
Sister Catherine to invent so improbable a tale?
What advantage could accrue to the Sister in thus
attempting by an extraordinary narrative to deceive
her director in whom she confided implicitly? Are
we to infer that she was impelled by self-love, by
vanity or ambition, or by the desire of esteem, that
having been the cynosure of all eyes during her
novitiate, she might rise rapidly to honorable rank
in the Community? Evidence, which after all is
said, is the test of truth, is against these implica-
tions, for no such thoughts ever entered her mind.
The Inquiry has demonstrated that on the occasion
of the first interview with her director, relative to
the vision, she exacted of him the formal promise
never to reveal her name or identity. That her
secret remained her own is all the more marvelous
inasmuch as she was placed in an establishment
whose personnel numbered one hundred fifty—
sisters and novices, among whom she was ever

apprehensive of not merely being discovered but even suspected. Nothing that the promoter might adduce can render the Sister more secure against prejudice than her own absolute will to remain unknown and its perfect accomplishment."

The silence of Sister Catherine is a proof of her humility and consequently of her sincerity. Many persons, especially Daughters of Charity, who came in contact with our Blessed Sister, were struck with the purity which beamed in her countenance and the frankness that exhaled from her speech. Her face bore the impress of modesty. "Her eyes of a limpid blue were the very embodiment of candor," writes one who knew her well. When the Servant of God spoke her very accents betokened unaffected sincerity. One day during recreation a young Sister playfully remarked that "of a truth the Sister who believed she had seen the Blessed Virgin, had beheld only a picture." "My dear," replied Sister Catherine in tones so emphatic that the incident remains indelibly impressed on the minds of those present, "my dear, the Sister who saw the Blessed Virgin saw her in

86

the flesh just as we see each other." This said, she sank back into her habitual silence and the conversation turned on other subjects.

In truth the uprightness of the young Sister cannot be called into question. But in the impossibility of doubt, and in fact no one does doubt that Sister Catherine believed firmly that she saw and heard what she affirms, may it not be proved that she was the victim of an optical or an auricular illusion, of a religious and mystical hallucination?

This second phase of the problem now claims our most earnest attention.

In the first place the daughter of Pierre Labouré was by no means the sport of a nervous temperament, of an over-excited imagination. No antecedent circumstances rendered this child of Fain-les-Moutiers susceptible to the aberrations of ill-directed piety or false mysticism. Indeed in reviewing the twenty-four years of her laborious life, passed far from the feverish atmosphere of cities, those restless centers where nervous affections of all sorts are engendered, we encounter no indication of any such derangement. On the contrary the estimate

87

of the Seer as gleaned from the notes of the Directress of the Seminary, Rue du Bac, in 1830, reads thus: "Catherine Labouré—medium height, strong, intelligent, judgment moderate, pious and earnest in the practice of virtue." Might not this appreciation be predicated of the average novice in any community? Moreover these notes are confirmed by the testimony of Father Aladel, the director of her conscience. Witness his responses when the Council of Inquiry in 1836 put the following questions concerning the young Sister:

"Was there not something extraordinary in her devotion?"

"No," he replied "her piety was then, as it is now, simple and straightforward."

"Has an especial devotion to the Mother of God been remarked in her?"

"Her devotion to the Mother of God has never been manifested in such a way as to attract attention, still I know full well that she had great confidence in the Blessed Virgin."

"Is the young woman simple and candid?"

"Exdeedingly so—there is absolutely nothing extraordinary about her."

"Does she betray an over-excited imagination?"

"No, on the other hand, she is cool and even naturally apathetic."

Such a nature is hardly predisposed to nervous disorders. We have besides Sister Catherine's own opinion on visions and alleged miracles. "I will tell you," she wrote in 1844, "that it grieves me very much to note in all, nearly all your letters that you speak of miracles, as if the good God would work them for trifling causes. Wretched creatures as we are, how expect God to operate miracles in our behalf! You even relate one after you left the Community. Alas! only God knows whether or not it is a miracle. Did our Lord, the Blessed Mother and the saints publish the miracles they effected? Where is our humility? How far short of theirs it falls! Let us rather say that we are destitute of that virtue."

In Sister Catherine we find traces neither of presumptuous pride nor of exaggerated enthusiasm.

89

The Servant of God so far from possessing a temperament favorable to the development of hallucinations, does not even manifest the slightest symptons discernible in its victims. Indeed the characteristics of the apparitions are absolutely foreign to those which distinguish the visions of the hallucinated.

Let us now consider Sister Catherine before, during, and after the Manifestation of November 27, 1830.

In the first place, it requires for the production of an hallucination a combination of circumstances whose occurrence determines it infallibly as such. What circumstances were necessary to yield the apparition under discussion?

"It is not in the darkness of the night," says the Reporter of the Canonical Inquiry, "not during sleep that the above described picture appears, not in a dream is it viewed, not even one of those dreams, truly heavenly visions with which according to Holy Writ God has at times favored His servants. No, it is in the full light of day, in the Chapel of the Community, during Mass or during

THE MANIFESTATION

meditation that the event happens—in a place and at a time when enjoying the full use of her senses, the entire freedom of her faculties—that the Sister beholds the picture, notes all it represents, reads the inscribed prayer, hears accurately the order given and the promise made and reports all with precision of detail.

Again, after the attacks the victim of hallucination exhibits a twofold depression, that of the will and that of the intellect, and in proportion as the disposition manifests irritability and insubordination, so does the mind become incapable of reasoning, of coherence and an undisturbed line of thought. But the Inquiry of 1836 especially emphasizes the remarkable submission of Sister Catherine to her director, Father Aladel. Though fully convinced of the reality of her visions, still persuaded that her director will deem the revelation she has made a sport of the imagination, the Sister no longer ventures to discuss the subject with him. Nevertheless she never disclosed to any other what had occured. The Report emphasizes the humility, obedience and force of character which such conduct implies. A soul less heroic, one abandoned to caprice, would have undoubtedly referred the matter to more lenient judges, to several tribunals perhaps.

After refuting the first consideration, we now turn to her long life in the Community in support of the second. During the forty-six years after the manifestation, Sister Catherine gave evidence of an intellect vigorous and clear which however, her scanty education and lack of culture concealed from prejudiced and shallow minds. It is true that a mere glance at the writings of the Seer, at the accounts of the apparitions, retreat notes, etc., will hardly convince such. But examine attentively the book of accounts wherein Sister Catherine entered the receipts and expenditures entailed in her humble office in the poultry yard, a charge which was hers at the Hospital of Enghien. The remarkable neatness of the register which though in use for thirty years, has the appearance of newness, the markedly characteristic handwriting, the entries wherein naught save orthography is slighted, the regularity of the truth-telling figures worthy of

THE MANIFESTATION

the approbation of the most rigid economist, do not all these qualities typify clearness of intellect, orderly precision and a well-balanced mind? What a contrast to the incomprehensible statements, incoherent passages, interrupted sentences in which the writings of the hallucinated abound! Moreover the behavior of the Seer of Rue du Bac at the time of the apparitions differ essentially from that of the unhappy visionary.

Let us cite two prominent distinctions. In the case of the hallucinated the imagination always retains cloudy and evanescent ideas. The forms they see are wavering and indeterminate, whereas the narrative of our Sister is characterized by that wealth of detail and accuracy of description already noted. For example, consider merely the Manifestation of November twenty-seventh: the date and place of the apparition, the attire, the height, the countenance, the expression, the hands, the rays, etc., all is observed, determined and minutely reproduced in words. "Here" concludes the Promoter of the Canonical Inquiry, "there is no question of one of those trifling visions which like meteors are beheld for an instant and then vanish forever."

Again the hallucinated make no discovery, neither invent nor create but simply remember and in exercising the memory often more or less unconsciously construct forms already in actual existence. But the Seer of Rue du Bac delineates an absolutely new type of Madonna which her memory and imagination could never have contributed either in conceiving the details or in arranging the whole. This we would develop in the third part of this exposition, in what might be styled the symbolism of the Manifestation of November twenty-seventh.

The author of a remarkable treatise on the Blessed Virgin under the unpretentious title of "Essays on Theology in Art" writes: "Christian art has ever recognized that category of representations wherein are assembled as in a panorama the various prerogatives of the Immaculate Virgin. Of this number is the Madonna commonly called 'of the Miraculous Medal.'" In the course of his work the Abbé Broussolle frequently accentuates

94

the artistic value of the representations of the Virgin of 1830.

Borrowing the thought of the Reverend Abbé we shall endeavor to show that the Manifestation of 1830 presents to the view a manifold symbolism and is moreover unique since the Immaculate Virgin is represented under an entirely novel aspect, in loveliness transcendent and supernatural or as Sister Catherine put it "all beauty in beauty supreme."

But what are the glorious privileges symbolized by the apparition of November 27, 1830? The first apparition of Mary to Sister Catherine Labouré shows her, standing, her foot victoriously crushing the head of the serpent. In the light of the most ancient and best authorized theology this attitude is the fittest symbol of the triumph of the Mother of God over the demon. Moreover the invocation traced in letters of gold around the picture, explicitly designates Mary "conceived without sin." Such is the first mystery proclaimed by the Manifestation. And yet the author of "The History and Theory of Religious Symbolism of both the

95

Old and the New Dispensation" does not hesitate
to write in 1871: "Our age which has had the
good fortune of seeing realized through the instru-
mentality of the illustrious Pontiff the desires of
so many centuries concerning the dogma of the
Immaculate Conception, has discovered with the
proclamation of this article of faith, that sacred
iconography is incomplete inasmuch as it lacks a
representation of what was at first merely a pious
belief, but later the article of faith henceforth insep-
arable from the Blessed Virgin.   We are forced
to admit that the early attempts proved failures
since in the search for something novel, the result
was the lifeless representation of a woman with
hands outstretched as imaged on the medal styled
Miraculous.   Happily upon the latter the serpent is
represented under the heel of the Virgin, thus
symbolizing one of the ideas which the Immaculate
Conception of the woman destined to triumph over
Satan by the one indispensable condition of never
having been under his influence, should reveal."

To the objections of the Abbé Auber we shall
oppose the opinions not only of a critic of art but a

theologian as well, whom we have already cited. Like the Virgin of Lourdes, the symbolic image of 1830 seems to Father Broussolle to establish "very effectually from the viewpoint of the needs of piety, the title of 'Immaculate Conception' to which we should give our strict adherence. . . . A Madonna presented with the serpent under her feet is a most praiseworthy image of the Immaculate, since it recalls the action which expressly demonstrates this privilege." This iconographic title of Mary, "Eve crushing the head of the serpent," he considers incontestable since it is warranted by the very words of the promise of the prerogative in the proto-announcement of the Immaculate Conception.

Some have taken exception to the image of 1830 and have asked: "Why is the august Mother deprived of her Son from whom she derives all her glory and who is universally acknowledged the essential cause of her happiness? "Assuredly" they say, "this mystery is but ill-understood since to give it proper expression existing iconography should be constrained to undergo no change either in virtue of augmentation or diminution. And all down the ages from the first apparition of this heavenly Virgin, has not the Mother been ever portrayed, the Divine Child pressed to her bosom or reposing on her blessed lap?" Could it be that the Manifestation of 1830 was destined to undermine the edifice erected under the guidance of the Holy Spirit? Far from it. On the contrary the Immaculate Virgin of Rue du Bac instead of impairing the beautiful tradition of the past has become the complement and the crown thereof. In other words the Immaculate Conception in the entire symbolism of the Manifestation of 1830, is interwoven with two other privileges which unite most intimately the Mother of God with her Divine Son. The development of this statement is our direct reply to the illiberal critics above quoted.

The second prerogative manifested to Sister Catherine is the efficacious intercession of the Most Holy Virgin. What office does Mary hold in Heaven? Is she not our intercessor, the dispensatrix too of those graces which she herself has obtained for us by her all-powerful petition? Has she not vouchsafed to evidence this in a sensible manner in the apparition to Catherine Labouré in two distinct attitudes, that of prayer when she holds in her hands and presses close to her heart a globe soliciting at the same time the divine mercy in favor of the world, and again as Queen whose extended hands laden with graces, are an invitation to all to approach with confidence and to participate in this wealth of treasure?

Not only the fact but the manner and extent of Mary's intercession are symbolized in the apparition of 1830. In her hands the Virgin holds a globe surmounted by a small gold cross, and prays the while to her Divine Son. Mark the role of Mary in the distribution of graces, how she unites her intercession, an intercession actual even though dependent, with that of Jesus Christ. With regard to the intercession of the Most Holy Virgin, theologians differ as to its universality. Bossuet holds that God having once willed to give us Jesus Christ by the Blessed Virgin, "the gifts of God being without repentance," this order obtains. It is and ever will be true? This is a fundamental principle which we deem worthy of reiteration, namely, that having received through Mary's charity the universal principle of grace, through her mediation we receive also its various applications in all the conditions which the Christian life imposes. Since her maternal charity has contributed so largely to our salvation in the mystery of the Incarnation, the universal source of grace, so too will she eternally use her influence in all those other operations which are but its attendants.

The voice heard by Sister Catherine Labouré utters the same truth: "My child, this globe which you see, represents the entire world, especially France and each person in particular." Mark the statement, "the entire world, especially France and each person in particular." Then the picture turns and the reverse conveys a message truly eloquent as the voice gives expression thereto: "The M and the two hearts say enough." The M surmounted by a cross and the two hearts side by side adorned with the emblems of the Passion seem to designate the ineffable mystery of the Coredemption.

Now according to the teaching of His Holiness Pius X in his encyclical for the fiftieth anniversary of the proclamation of the dogma of the Immaculate Conception: "There existed between Jesus and His Mother so intimate a union of life and suffering that the words of the Prophet are applicable to both: 'My life is wasted with grief and my years with sighs.' The Virgin stood at the foot of the cross stricken doubtless with the awful spectacle, still happy inasmuch as her Divine Son was immolating Himself for the human race, sharing His torments withal to such an extent that if the thing were possible, she would have infinitely preferred to suffer in His stead." The Holy Father concludes thus: "Owing to this union of sentiment and suffering Mary merits to be associated in the restoration of fallen humanity and, by consequence, the title of dispensatrix of all the treasures Jesus has acquired for us by His death." Was not this special participation of the Most Holy Virgin in the redemption recognized by Sister Catherine on the reverse of the picture of the great Manifestation?

Immaculate Conception, potent intercession, ineffable coredemption—triple aureola that adorned the Mother of God on that one day November 27,

1830! Affirming the same privilege, no other than that of the mediation of Mary, how these mysteries blend in the unity of one symbolism!

It must be understood that the idea of mediation is applicable to Mary only in a secondary sense, our Lord Jesus is in the strict sense of the word, the sole Pontiff and Mediator of the New Law. It is in Him, with Him and by Him that our homages are accepted, that our prayers must mount to God. It is by Him, with Him and in Him that graces are dispensed to us and descend from God to us. If, however, one should read the epistle to the Hebrews which treats of the mediation of our Lord Jesus Christ, reflecting meanwhile on the three prerogatives of the Blessed Virgin revealed by the Manifestation of 1830—all restrictions safely guarded—one will immediately be inclined to attribute some of the characteristics of this mediation to the Madonna of Rue du Bac.

Says the Apostle in the epistle mentioned above:

"For it was fitting we should have such a high priest," firstly, "holy, innocent, undefiled, separated

102

from sinners and made higher than the heavens;" secondly, "One who is seated on the right hand of the throne of the Divine Majesty, as minister of the Sanctuary and of the true Tabernacle, always living to make intercession for us;" and thirdly: "One who needed not daily to offer sacrifices, first for His own sins and then for the people's; for this He did once in offering Himself." In this mediation in the economy of the redemption wrought by our Lord Jesus Christ, may we not assert that the Immaculate Virgin occupies a chosen place and that as such she is revealed in the Manifestation of 1830?

On the very eve of the apparition to Sister Catherine, the Abbé Gerbet, future Bishop of Perpignan, published his "Considerations on the Regenerating Dogma of Catholic Piety." In the chapter treating of the social life of the Church, he thus expresses the idea of the Priesthood: "This institution adheres to an order of ideas superior to that which generally impresses such intellects as are inclined to consider external effects rather than to penetrate into the essence of things. The priest

is regarded under the touching epithets of Father
of the poor, Consoler of the afflicted, Confident
of overburdened consciences, but this aureola of
charity which is the essential ornament of the
sacerdotal character, is not its elemental characteristic. The fundamental idea of the sacerdotal office
is that of mediation." Neither should we view the
Blessed Virgin solely under the unique aspect of
her radiant and maternal goodness, but consider
her, moreover, in one of her distinctive features,
that of mediation.

Now, the idea of mediation is passive and active
according as there is question of effect or of cause
in the work of redemption. In virtue of the first
privilege manifested to Sister Catherine Labouré,
the Blessed Virgin holds a "preëminent position in
passive mediation." Mary is conceived without sin
in consequence of a "preservative redemption;" the
Virgin is "redeemed by the anticipated merits of
Jesus Christ," and the Immaculate Conception is
"the fruit of this special redemption." The
"sublime and extraordinary redemption of Mary
accomplished and expressed in her Immaculate

104

Conception" is closely allied to the work of the
redemption by Jesus Christ. It is indeed its crown,
the type of all other redemptions. It is in the
sense of this passive mediation that in the "Little
Office of the Immaculate Conception" approved
by Pius IX, we are permitted to salute the august
Mother of God:

> "*Terra es benedicta et sacerdotalis*
> *Sancta et immunis culpae originalis.*"
> "Thou land set apart from uses profane
> And free from the curse which in Adam began."

Again, Mary occupies an analogous position in
active mediation, that is, as coredemptrix, and the
practically indispensable treasurer of all the graces
Jesus Christ has merited for us. Does not the
Virgin of Rue du Bac appear under these two
aspects? On the one hand she is likened to the
priest, "to him who dispenseth sacred things, who
becometh the mediator between God and man,
between God from whom he receives and man to
whom he dispenses; between God to whom he
offers gifts and man to whom he is appointed to
present them." Is not this the attitude of the

105

Virgin most powerful, who after she presents the globe to God immediately extends towards man her virginal hands all radiant with graces? Then the reverse of the apparition—does it not clearly indicate the Virgin Coredemptrix, "who at the foot of the Cross while the Lamb without spot was immolating Himself freely for the salvation of the world, sacrificed herself for the same end, and so performed in union with Him the office of the supreme Priesthood?"

A theologian has written: "In the first ages of Christianity the idea of associating Mary in the sacrifice of her Son was thoroughly appreciated. The most holy Virgin was pictured clothed in sacerdotal vestments offering Him to God for the salvation of the world. Later on, this thought as true as it is beautiful, found less favor in art, and now and then, Mary is represented swooning at the foot of the Cross. Christian art should energetically refute this false conception, for during the sacrifice of Calvary, the bearing of the Blessed Mother was preëminently sacerdotal. Was it not then her mediation both passive and active, in

106

THE MANIFESTATION

Heaven and at the foot of the Cross, that Mary manifested to Blessed Sister Catherine Labouré in 1830? Should we not believe too that it is in the sense of this privilege, so glorious to the Blessed Virgin, that the progress foreseen by Père Gratry will see fulfilled?

The author of the "Month of Mary of the Immaculate Conception" to which Cardinal Perraud assigns the place of honor among the numerous productions of this nature yearly published, writes: "In an humble sanctuary at Rome, preserved for more than a century, lies the body of Blessed Leonard of Port Maurice. Beside it exposed for the veneration of the faithful, is an autograph letter of the holy man, which treats of the Immaculate Conception, and affirms that when the light of this capital truth shall shine in all its splendor, that is, when the Immaculate Conception shall have been defined as an article of faith, the same moment will witness the advent of tranquillity and peace throughout the world." Père Gratry continues: "This prophecy may be contested, still we may in all safety adhere to the harmony and depth of the happy convictions expressed in the inspired letter of the holy man, namely 'the world shall not abide forever in its present state of confusion; it must be governed in justice and peace and truth, and this will be effected by the influence of Christian wisdom and piety, by developing and exalting the glorious privileges, merits and dignity of the Immaculate Virgin, Mother of the Word Incarnate.' "

It is not perhaps impossible to foresee in what manner "this extraordinary development of devotion to the Blessed Virgin," predicted by various saints as the outcome of the definition of the dogma of the Immaculate Conception, exhibit itself.

CHAPTER V

WHILE the plan of the biography of Sister Catherine Labouré should by no means include the complete history of the Miraculous Medal, still the life of the Servant of God during this period is so closely allied to the events appertaining to the production and propagation of the medal that her career is best interpreted in the light of these events. The first consequence of the apparition of 1830 was that Sister Catherine was charged with the commission to have struck and disseminated the medal which was so soon to win for itself the appellation "Miraculous."

On the expiration of the term of her seminary, our Blessed Sister was stationed at the Hospital of Enghien, recently transferred to the Faubourg Saint Antoine, Rue Picpus, Paris This hospital was founded in 1819 by the Duchess of Bourbon in memory of her son, the Duke of Enghien. Destined to serve as a home for aged women, it admitted convalescents who were forced to quit the hospitals of Paris, and later on domestics and the widows of domestics of the Houses of Orleans and Condé. In the year 1831 seven Daughters of Charity devoted themselves to the care of the fifty inmates of the establishment.

Before going to her destination Sister Catherine passed a few days at one of the large institutions of Paris. Father Aladel, the director of her conscience, also contrived to repair thither. The rumor of the visions had circulated and he was known to be the recipient of the confidence of the favored Sister. He no sooner appeared, therefore, than the Sisters gathered round and assailed him with questions. He thus describes the situation:

"I scarcely knew how to extricate myself from the dilemma, how to answer without betraying my embarrassment or the Sister's confidence. Trusting in the assistance of Mary, I related quite simply the facts connected with the prodigy, marveling meanwhile at what I witnessed, for the good Sister whose confusion I dreaded was perfect mistress of herself, participated in the conversation with the same liberty of spirit as the others without a change of attitude or countenance being perceptible, and spoke of the event as if it had concerned another. I accordingly concluded that the guarding of the secret was agreeable to the Lord and that His benediction attended the silence and humility which the favored one had made her refuge."

Upon reaching the hospital Sister Catherine was employed in the kitchen. In the obscurity of this duty it was an easy matter to conceal from all, the favors vouchsafed her. Early in August of the same year 1831, she received from her eldest sister, Sister Marie Louise, a letter replete with judicious counsel and excellent advice to guide her experiences in community life. It is obvious from this letter that the Superioress of Castelsarrasin was absolutely ignorant of the extraordinary graces bestowed on our Blessed Sister. We shall give the letter in full.

III

BLESSED CATHERINE LABOURÉ

My very dear Sister:

The grace of our Lord be forever with us!

Your dear letter and that of your worthy Superioress are at hand and I am most grateful for the interest she manifests in you. For your part, my loved one, endeavor by your good conduct to prove your gratitude. While I feel quite sure that you will never be the cause of anxiety to anybody, still this is not enough. You should give great consolation by applying to all your duties with simplicity, cheerfulness, diligence and openness of heart. Such dispositions are graces very necessary for us, and if we are destitute of them we should make strenuous efforts by fervent prayer to obtain them.

A Daughter of Charity truly charitable is amiable to all. On seeing her men say, "Behold a servant of God! What humility, compassion, forbearance and kindness mark her deportment!" Then they who thus gaze in admiration at the Daughter of Charity say within themselves: If God displays His goodness to such an extent in His

112

creatures, how thrilled we shall be when He reveals to us His own infinite perfections!" Happy the Daughters of Charity who bear this resemblance to God! He can refuse them nothing nor will He ever abandon them.

Let us examine, dear Zoé, whether we possess any of these traits of resemblance to the Divine Master. Must we not admit that we are but poor copyists capable only of spoiling all? But shall we on this account yield to discouragement? By no means. Let us acknowledge our insufficiency, our incapacity and say: "Behold, my God, of what I am capable. To Thee I offer my good will and all the happy dispositions Thou hast granted me. Accomplish Thy work and permit not that I be an obstacle thereto."

Now is the time for you to mould yourself to the functions of our holy state. Remember we are not to be our own guides, for we are blind regarding ourselves and might easily abandon the right path and follow the wrong. I have, however, little anxiety for you in this respect. You have a good Superioress who I feel sure has your entire confidence, and many companions whose experience is your safeguard. Consequently you enjoy every opportunity to form yourself to the spirit of our state. How I thank God for this favor!

I beg you to offer my respects to your worthy Superioress and to your dear companions, and for yourself ever prove good, obedient, open and considerate toward all. My companions send you affectionate messages and recommend themselves to your prayers. Pray for me as I do for you, and believe in my sincere affection,

Sister M. Louise

U. D. O. C.

There is one expression in the above letter which must have deeply impressed the Seer of Rue du Bac, viz., "My God, to Thee I offer my good will. Perfect Thou Thy work and permit not that I be an obstacle thereto." The work to which Sister Catherine was called, the mission entrusted to her by Heaven, was to have a medal struck commemorative of the apparition of 1830. Time and again had the Servant of God besought this favor of her confessor, yet Father Aladel continued deaf to her entreaties, regarding her communications as illusive, mere phantoms of the imagination.

After the third and last apparition the Blessed Virgin had said to her: "My daughter, henceforth you will see me no more, but you will hear my voice during meditation." Soon this voice made itself heard in the sad complaint: "The Blessed Virgin is not pleased with your negligence in having the medal struck." And in reply came Sister Catherine's gentle accusation: "My good Mother, you see he will not believe me."

"Be tranquil," replied the voice, "the day will come when he will do what I desire. He is my servant and should fear to displease me."

Not until the beginning of the year 1832, however, did Father Aladel, prompted by circumstances singularly providential, decide to comply with the wish of his penitent or rather with the mandate of the Blessed Virgin. He writes: "In an interview with the Most Reverend Hyacinthe de Quélen, Archbishop of Paris, an opportunity presented of relating the details of the apparition. The venerable prelate, far from seeing any impropriety in the production of the medal, deemed it on the contrary calculated to foster piety and devotion. He moreover expressed the desire to have one of the first medals struck. From this moment I resolved to have the medal cast but the ravages of the cholera having multiplied the functions of my ministry, the execution of my plan was deferred until June 1832, when the medal was produced according to the model sketched in the fourth chapter of the present work."

The English author of *"L'Epopée Mariale en France au XIXe Siècle,"* thus addresses the Catholic reader: "Consider attentively your medal of the Immaculate Conception, generally known as the Miraculous Medal. On its obverse is pictured the vision granted to Sister Catherine, the Immaculate Virgin, her extended hands laden with graces, and encircling the image the beautiful invocation 'O Mary conceived without sin, pray for us who have recourse to thee;' on the reverse the insignia already described, the monogram of Mary surmounted by a cross, and below, two hearts, the one crowned with thorns, the other pierced with a sword; finally twelve stars corresponding artistically to the invocation on the face."

An order for two thousand was filled toward the end of June 1832 by Vachette, Engraver, No. 54 Quai des Orfèvres. With deep veneration did Sister Catherine receive the holy medal merely observing that now it must be disseminated. The prime mover in the propagation as well as in its production was His Grace. Having learned that Mgr. de Praat, former Archbishop of Mechlin, was still obstinate toward the Church although in imminent danger of death, Archbishop de Quélen visited the invalid. Though at first repulsed by the poor wanderer, he was presently recalled and the prodigal child touched by grace deplored his errors and died reconciled to God. Such was the first conversion, the first prodigy wrought by the medal soon to be proclaimed "Miraculous" by the voice of the people.

Medals in great quantities and literature treating of the wondrous efficacy thereof began to be circulated with extraordinary rapidity. At the end

of a few months millions were cast and forwarded
to the most remote countries. Requests for the
medal came from Rome, from the various religious
orders that were most zealous in its distribution,
and it is said that the Holy Father, Gregory XVI,
bestowed it on many as a mark of pontifical favor
and placed one at the foot of his crucifix. With
the utmost avidity did the faithful of all ranks seek
the medal, "that protects and cures."

It was now deemed necessary to collect authenticated facts regarding these wonders and while
propagating the new devotion to safeguard the
faithful against inevitable counterfeits. The first
of these publications entitled, "Historical Notice of
the Origin and Effects of the New Medal" was the
product of Abbé Le Guillou. A resident of the
diocese of Quimper, he had come to Paris at the
recommendation of his bishop to edit some important documents and to establish a society of religious art. He died February 3, 1890, Titular
Canon of Paris, Member of the Committee on
Historic and Religious Chant, and Knight of the
Papal Order of Gregory the Great. He had re-

ceived tonsure at the hands of the archbishop and
in 1833 was appointed Chaplain of the Hospital
of Charity.

The "*Semaine Religieuse*" of the diocese of Paris
from which we have culled these notes states:
"Admiring the remarkable talents and theological
proficiency of the Abbé, Archbishop de Quélen
directed him to inquire into the circumstances of
the apparition of the Blessed Virgin to Sister
Catherine." The results of his first inquiry found
in his "*Notice Historique*" read thus: "There is
much comment at the present time especially in
Paris, regarding a miraculous medal of the Blessed
Virgin and very many prodigies are cited as having
been effected by its means in the provinces as well
as in the capital where it is worn with faith and
confidence in the power of the Virgin Mary.
Having examined with diligence the origin of the
medal and the circumstances of the most striking
miracles operated through its use, I am convinced
that I shall respond to the piety of the faithful by
sharing with them the results of my research.
They will doubtless be edified, consoled and

prompted to cast themselves with renewed fervor into the arms of her who seems to embrace mankind only to conquer man's ingratitude by her benefits. This medal exhibiting on one side the image of the Immaculate and on the other the letter M surmounted by a cross below which are the sacred hearts of Jesus and Mary, was revealed to a pious soul consecrated to God in one of the communities of Paris.

"Let me in the first place produce an extract from the letter of a worthy priest, the director of the good religious. It was my privilege to discourse at length with him upon the circumstances connected with the revelation of the medal and the wonderful conversions and cures that recommend it so powerfully to the piety of the faithful. I could not have drawn upon a better source of information and consequently I am deeply grateful for his courtesy in acquainting me with what he considered would redound to the honor of the most holy Virgin."

To appreciate the tenor of this document let the reader recall the irreligious character of the public

THE MIRACULOUS MEDAL

mind in 1830. Today after a period of uninterrupted prodigies effected by the Immaculate Mary, men are more or less familiar with the idea of supernatural intervention but the Voltairian and scoffing generation which succeeded the French Revolution was decidedly antagonistic to any such conception. Wherefore through the writings of Canon Le Guillou as well as those of Father Aladel there runs a strain of apology and anxiety for they felt restricted to make the least possible publicity of the apparition with which Sister Catherine was favored and merely remarked what was absolutely necessary for the authorization of the medal. The following extract which serves as a prelude to Father Aladel's letter as inserted in the "*Notice Historique*" will bear witness to this fact: "There is no reason for astonishment that the confessor should disclose what had been confided to him concerning the visions. The case in point treats merely of a praiseworthy matter. Authorization moreover was given the director by the religious to reveal all he should judge necessary to secure the production of the medal and inspire the confidence of the faithful. The name only of the favored individual was to remain a secret."

And now let us turn our attention to the narrative of the spiritual director of Sister Catherine: "Toward the latter part of 1830 Sister N, a novice of one of the communities of Paris devoted to the service of the poor, believed she had seen during prayer as in a tableau the Blessed Virgin, her attitude that of Mary under the title of Immaculate Conception. She appeared standing, her arms extended and her hands emitting rays of light. Then the Sister distinguished the words: 'These rays are symbols of the graces Mary obtains for men.' Around the image in golden letters was traced the invocation, 'O Mary conceived without sin, pray for us who have recourse to thee.' When the Sister had gazed on this picture for some time it appeared to turn and on the reverse she beheld the letter M surmounted by a cross and below, the sacred hearts of Jesus and Mary. Again the voice was heard: 'A medal must be struck after this model. Such as wear it indulgenced and recite devoutly the little prayer shall enjoy the especial protection of the Mother of God.'

"This person immediately communicated this fact to me but I candidly admit that I considered it the pure illusion of a pious imagination. In reply I limited myself to a few words of advice on true devotion to Mary and observed that imitation of her virtues was the surest method of honoring her and meriting her protection. Apparently there was no further question of what she had seen. After an interval of six months however the same vision was repeated. When informed thereof I still adhered to the first impressions and treated the Sister accordingly. Finally after the lapse of another six months she saw and heard for the third time the same things but the voice now added that the Blessed Virgin was not pleased owing to negligence in having the medal struck. I now viewed the matter as of importance, still I gave no outward expression to my thoughts. Indeed I experienced a certain fear of displeasing her whom the Church so justly styles the 'refuge of sinners.' "

Immediately following this letter is an exhorta-

123

tion by the author wherein he presses all those favored by Mary for their confidence in the medal to apprize him of any striking prodigies that had come under their observation. He even proposed publishing all well-authenticated facts hoping thereby to silence impiety. Many medical men had been constrained to recognize miraculous intervention in seemingly hopeless cases. Others who were determined not to yield their prejudices despite indisputable evidence, in their embarrassment exclaimed: "Truly this is phenomenal." They would gladly if possible attribute the marvels to the power of magnetism. How blind is the intellect of man when he wanders from the light of faith!

The "Notice" published first in his "Month of Mary" and afterward issued under separate cover in vast quantities, was reproduced in a work entitled "Novena to Mary to implore her assistance by wearing on one's person the medal recently struck in honor of her Immaculate Conception." The volume bears the imprimatur of the Archbishop of Paris under date of August 29, 1834 just

124

two years after the first production and dissemination of the emblem revealed to Sister Catherine.

In 1835 the artist Lecerf while working on the painting of the apparition of the Blessed Virgin now at the Seminary of Rue du Bac, in doubt as to the color of the veil, consulted Father Aladel who in turn questioned Sister Catherine in a general way about the apparition only to meet with this reply: "I cannot recall what I have seen. But one circumstance is clearly present, namely, that the veil of the Blessed Virgin was of auroral whiteness." Truly remarkable this statement since the only detail the Sister could give was precisely the one her director was seeking. One other instance of temporary amnesia in Sister Catherine is recorded. It occurred in presence of Father Etienne, Superior General, when the Seer declared that she had forgotten all the particulars of the apparition.

To meet Sister Catherine, to enjoy an interview with her had ever been the ardent desire of the Archbishop. He yielded however to the excuses presented by the director and passed out of this life without gazing upon the features of the Servant of God. His holy death occurred December 31, 1839.

During the years 1839—1841 the bishops of France emulated one another in soliciting and procuring of the Holy See privileges similar to those conceded to the Archbishop of Paris. And all the while the world knew not the name of Catherine Labouré. Indeed there was nothing in the Servant of God to distinguish her from her companions except a somewhat greater love of suffering and a keener attraction for the hidden life. A letter from the Superioress of Châtillon, the place of Sister Catherine's postulatum, bears witness to this. We shall give the letter in part.

"It was with real pleasure that I received your letter, my very dear Sister. I should have desired better news of your health; those sciatic pains have, I know, caused you great suffering. There you are at the very center of medical skill and unable to find a remedy. The Great Physician thus leads you to the practice of patience and submission to His good pleasure. I thank our

126

THE MIRACULOUS MEDAL

Lord for the sentiments of faith and love with which He has endowed you whereby you may amass so much merit for eternity. Yes, my dear Sister, let us supplicate this good Father to grant us the grace to glorify Him no matter with what trials He may see fit to afflict us. It is in this sense that I accept the good wishes that you offer. They are precious coming from one whom I esteem so highly. It is my affection for you that prompts those I frame for your progress in virtue."

The above letter is dated January 11, 1841. At the end of the same year a young woman of Russian extraction and noble birth, brought up in the schismatical Greek Church, was spending some time in Paris. During her sojourn she was introduced at the House of the Daughters of Charity where she was destined to pass so many years and to have all the aspirations of her soul gratified. This was Natalie Narischkin soon to be known as Sister Natalie, Daughter of Charity of Saint Vincent de Paul. From the interesting life of Sister Natalie entitled "A Sister's Story" by Mrs. Augustus Craven, we cull the following:

BLESSED CATHERINE LABOURÉ

"Among all the churches of Paris none had more attraction for Natalie than the chapel of that monastery where recently had taken place the wonderful vision commemorated by the Miraculous Medal. The humble Sister who had been selected as the messenger of happy tidings was living at this time but her name was unknown. Quietly moving among her companions, nothing betrayed her extraordinary calling. While the devotion which was to effect such marvels was gaining way throughout the world the Sister remained in her chosen obscurity, hidden like unseen flowers embalming the air though sheltered by their foliage from observation. Natalie listened with lively interest to every detail of the miraculous favor and for the first time penetrated the sense of the word humility in the plenitude of its meaning as taught by the Church and the practice of the saints." From this epoch is dated her conversion to the Catholic faith.

A little later, January 1842, a still more signal conversion attracted attention to the Manifestation of 1830, that of the instantaneous and perfect

conversion from Judaism of Alphonse Marie Ratis-
bonne. And because it is honorable to reveal and
confess the works of God, His Eminence, Cardinal
Patrizi, for the greater glory of God and the increase of devotion toward His Mother, is pleased
to allow this signal miracle to be published."

In consideration of this decree the Sacred Congregation of Rites granted, July 23, 1894, the
institution of the Feast of the Manifestation of the
Virgin Immaculate or of the Miraculous Medal, a
concession similar to that granted to the Holy
Rosary and the Scapular of Mount Carmel. November twenty-seventh has been appointed for this
feast.

CHAPTER VI

THE TWO FAMILIES OF SAINT VINCENT DE PAUL

1843—1846

IN the estimation of a writer who has made a deep study of the maze of vicissitudes experienced by the Sons of Saint Vincent, "the nineteenth century was for the Congregation of the Mission an epoch of extraordinary fecundity and expansion." Analogous though far more extensive prosperity characterized the Company of Daughters of Charity, the other religious family established by Saint Vincent. The well-spring of this uncommon progress was purely and simply the apparitions of 1830. That the favored one was cognizant of this influence and its effects is gathered from her detached notes written at various times. How she rejoices in the gradual development of the two families of Saint Vincent de Paul and seeks in prayer the means of hastening the day of complete regeneration!

THE TWO FAMILIES OF SAINT VINCENT

Read the following outbursts of fervor. "The family of Saint Vincent favored by this signal privilege!" "How many missionaries, how great the number of Daughters of Charity!" It is incontestable that from 1830 to 1843 the Congregation of the Mission despite all obstacles and notwithstanding an interior crisis which threatened its very existence, was distinguished by an enormous growth and strength, while for the Daughters of Charity the memorable event of the Manifestation of the Immaculate Virgin was the harbinger of astonishing good fortune. Not the most renowned sanctuary may take precedence over the modest chapel which the Queen of Heaven deigned to grace with her august presence. Attracted thither by an irresistible charm, innumerable generations of Christian virgins will under Mary's protection seek to clothe themselves with the livery of the Servants of the Poor, and this interpid army of charity penetrating even the most remote lands will prove the joy of the Church and the admiration of the world.

But let us return to Sister Catherine's reflections.

What a striking concurrence with this prodigous progress is manifest in the aspirations of the Servant of God for the perfect restoration of the spirit of Saint Vincent! With this one thought—eagerness for renovation—the mind of the humble Daughter of Charity seemed habitually preoccupied. Note her method. She desires first to be renewed herself in the spirit of her state. After a conference on the holy name of Mary she writes: "I shall consider her as my model at the beginning of all my actions, asking myself if Mary were to perform this act how would she do it and with what intention. How beautiful and consoling is the name of Mary! Mary!"

During the retreat of May 1839 the following resolutions were entered: "I shall offer myself to God without reserve bearing all annoyances and contradictions in a spirit of humility and penance. If He wills me to be in a state of humiliation, may His holy name be blessed! I offer myself to Him. . . . . .O Immaculate Heart of Mary, obtain for me the faith and love that attached you to the cross of Jesus Christ!" And again: "We believe

132

in thee, O holy Cross, we offer thee our act of reparation. Thou art our hope. Sanctify the just and convert sinners. O Mary, take pity on us!" What intense fervor animated the Servant of God when she wrote May seventeenth 1839: "O Mary, Mary, Mary, pray, pray, pray for us poor sinners now and at the hour of our death. . . . . Mary, O Mary!" Thus we see that Sister Catherine considered the time of retreat an opportunity for immense growth in holiness.

In 1842 the spiritual exercises of the retreat were conducted by Father Etienne. Anent the instruction on our Holy Rules the Sister writes: "To observe our rules well we must possess their spirit and not stop short at the letter of them. If we are attentive in the observance of little things we shall be prepared for greater in imitation of our Lord who should ever be our model. . . . O Jesus! O Mary!" The subject of another conference "The spirit of our state and the means to acquire it" gave expression to this beautiful petition: "It is by uniting the offices of Martha and Mary. . . . . O Mary, enable me to understand what it is to be a good Daughter of Charity and to penetrate the meaning of the spirit of our holy vows!" The conference on Chastity suggested the following resolution: "To watch most carefully over myself that I may not sully holy purity, frequently recalling to mind that chastity is the ornament of virgins. Without it a Daughter of Charity will not be saved. . . . . . In my temptations and aridity I shall always have recourse to Mary who is the essence of purity. . . O Mary conceived without sin!"

As a result of the retreat preached in May 1843 by Father Aladel, the supernatural horizon of Sister Catherine seems to be marked by greater scope. Henceforward she does not restrict her petitions to her individual needs but embraces all in her charity, especially the double family of Saint Vincent. This will be obvious from the subjoined considerations: "Month of Mary, twenty-fifth day: First instruction: Mary stands at the foot of the Cross. She is our model. In our trials let us also go to the foot of the cross and there after the example of Mary, deposit our afflictions. Let us entreat through her intercession all the graces we need."

"Month of Mary, twenty-ninth day: Mary has been assumed into Heaven! What ineffable glory! She is seated at the right hand of the King of kings! What an honor! She has received the fruit of the Holy Spirit, perseverance. We too must presevere in well doing, in fidelity to our resolutions after the example of Mary. Mary is before the throne of the Adorable Trinity. The Eternal Father clothes her with the sun; the moon is beneath her feet; and on her head rests a diadem of twelve stars. Thus has God exalted her, making her Queen of angels and of men. Ah! thrice welcome the moment when we too shall be admitted into that celestial abode! What happiness for us if we reach the blessed goal! O Mary!" It is noteworthy that throughout her papers there is not the merest mention of the favor of 1830. The secret of the apparitions is kept, as it were even from herself.

"Month of Mary, thirtieth day: On this day, it is fitting that we offer to the holy Virgin, all the resolutions formed during the month. Let us deposit our gift in her own sanctuary, her immacu-

135

late heart, the cherished temple wherein the divine Savior willed to dwell. O Immaculate Heart of Mary, obtain for us this grace through the merits of thy well-beloved Son!"

We insert in full the spiritual bouquet offered to the Blessed Virgin on the last day of the month: "May thirty-first: Resolved to pass no day without practising some virtue of which the Immaculate has given the example. This will not be difficult since our dear vocation affords us the opportunities in the works it bids us perform. O Immaculate Heart of Mary, obtain this grace for the two families of Saint Vincent!"

On the fourth day of the following August the general assembly of the Priests of the Mission elected as Superior General of their Congregation and of the Daughters of Charity, Rev. J. B. Etienne, a man destined by Providence to restore the work of Saint Vincent de Paul. Have we not reason to believe that the sacrifices of our Blessed Sister united to the prayers of Saint Vincent and the powerful mediation of Mary concurred in the choice of Father Etienne, so justly styled the

136

THE TWO FAMILIES OF SAINT VINCENT

Second Founder of the two families of Saint Vincent?

On September eighth 1843 the newly elected Superior General announced his appointment to the Daughters of Charity: "I am greatly encouraged, my dear Sisters, when I reflect under whose auspices I am to begin the exercise of my ministration in your regard. Neither am I insensible to the especial intervention of the august and Immaculate Mary who has so lovingly enriched you with extraordinary pledges of her tenderness. Undoubtedly it is the application of the merit of her dolors to our ills that has achieved their cure. It is her powerful mediation that has procured from God that our two families should not perish though encompassed by evil and that moreover He should make them His instruments in reanimating faith. To what cause other than this can we attribute the numerous vocations to your state, the marvelous and consoling development of your Company in the midst of storms and agitations?"

To the Priests of the Mission Father Etienne expresses himself in similar terms: "Am I not peculiarly authorized to entertain great confidence in the august and Immaculate Mary who has so recently displayed in our favor the grace of her protection? It is assuredly the merit of her sorrows that has terminated our misfortune and only through her intercession shall we be enabled to preserve the peace vouchsafed us.

"What a happy coincidence that our general assembly should end on the feast of her glorious Assumption. It is in her heart so pure and loving we have deposited our resolutions and our hopes. It would be impossible to convey the sentiments of delight that flooded my soul upon viewing the representatives of the Congregation prostrate at her feet, pronounce together the act of consecration used in the Company."

The origin of the act by which the Congregation yearly on the feast of the Assumption chooses Mary for protectress may be traced to August 15, 1662, just two years after the death of Saint Vincent. As early as 1658 the Daughters of Charity pronounced on the feast of the Immaculate Conception an act of almost identical content.

"We, most unworthy Daughters of Charity, in the presence of God and of the whole heavenly court, acknowledging the great need we have of the divine assistance, supplicate the, O Most Holy Virgin, who art all powerful with thy divine Son, to obtain for us the graces necessary to correct our defects; to acquire the virtues of our state and to discharge faithfully the duties of our holy vocation.

"Prostrate before thee, O Mother of Mercy, we most humbly conjure thee to accept the irrevocable offering we make to thee of our souls, of our bodies and our entire being, on this glorious feast of thy Immaculate Conception whereby we consecrate ourselves to thy love and service during the whole course of our life and for all eternity; purposing with the aid of the Holy Spirit, ever to show thee marked respect and veneration, and to induce others to serve, honor, imitate and invoke thee, that they may thereby render themselves pleasing and acceptable to Almighty God. We

139

also entreat thee, O Immaculate Virgin, to receive us all, and each one in particular, under thy maternal protection, while we acknowledge thee as our sovereign, our patroness and our advocate; beseeching thee to obtain pardon for the faults we have committed against the divine Majesty, and for our negligence in thy service, also that the members of the little Company of the Daughters of Charity may ever regard thee as their true and only Mother and ever experience thy gracious assistance in the practice of the virtues of charity, simplicity and patience and all the other virtues of their state; especially chastity, by protecting them against the dangers to which they may be exposed.

"We supplicate thee, O tender Mother. to obtain for us the grace to continue faithful in the service of the sick poor, and in the other duties in which we are employed; obtain for us also union among ourselves; fidelity in the observance of our Holy Rules, and final perseverance in our holy vocation; that, having faithfully served and imitated thy beloved Son in this life, we may with thee, praise and bless Him during all eternity. Amen"

THE TWO FAMILIES OF SAINT VINCENT

It is to the Blessed Louise de Marillac whose devotion to the Blessed Virgin was the distinguishing characteristic of her piety that we are indebted for this beautiful act. "Would to God" she wrote in all the fervor of her loving heart, "that I might make known the thoughts His goodness has communicated to me concerning the Immaculate Conception of the Blessed Virgin Mary. In time and in eternity I desire to love and honor her in every possible way." It is she too who has given us this prayer so dear to the Daughters of Charity. "Most Holy Virgin, I believe and confess thy holy and Immaculate Conception pure and without stain. O most pure Virgin, by thy virginal purity, thy Immaculate Conception, thy glorious prerogative of Mother of God, obtain for me of thy divine Son humility, charity, great purity of heart, body and mind, holy perseverance in my dear vocation, the gift of prayer, a good life and a happy death." And that other prayer: "O my God, may the perfection of the holy soul of Mary united to her body, be, I entreat Thee, comprehended by all creatures that they may admire and adore Thy almighty power and glorify Thee eternally for her all pure and Immaculate Conception. It is true, Holy Virgin, that thou wast ever preserved from the taint of sin by the merits of the Incarnation, the Passion and death of God's Son and thine. Thou art truly the eldest daughter of the Cross. Have compassion, therefore, O Mother of Mercy, on all souls redeemed by the Precious Blood of thy divine Son. Consider also, in view of God's glory the needs of the clergy and above all of Christ's Vicar on earth. Extend to them thy powerful succor. Obtain that we thy clients may glorify God in His essential beatitude and enjoy also the accidental bliss which thy amiable and loving presence will impart to the blessed in the state of glory.''

The Church recognizing this personal devotion of Saint Vincent de Paul and of Blessed Louise de Marillac toward Mary conceived without sin, declares in the office of the Miraculous Medal, that faithful to the traditions of the Holy Founder, the Congregation of the Mission has always rendered homage to the Immaculate Conception

THE TWO FAMILIES OF SAINT VINCENT

To point out the providential consequences of these traditions, in the favors conferred on Sister Catherine Labouré, was not the only concern of Father Etienne in 1843. He sought, moreover, to maintain the ancient customs and increase the practices of piety toward her who had shown herself so liberal in 1830.

Ever devoted and tenderly maternal toward the two families of Saint Vincent de Paul, Mary had during the apparitions of the month of July 1830, designated to Sister Catherine certain abuses that had found entrance into the Community, owing doubtless, to the misfortunes of the times. The new Superior was by no means unmindful of this fact. One year after his election, August 1844, Father Etienne addressed to the Daughters of Charity a circular esteemed by his historian one of the happiest efforts of his wisdom and experience. It is said that Sister Catherine through the medium of Father Aladel was the inspiration of the reforms urged by Father Etienne. This is nowhere more apparent than in the letter to which we allude, an extensive letter which embraces in its forty pages a series of recommendations and advices and which wrought such a revival of the primitive spirit in the Company. To substantiate our statement we cite a letter written by Sister Catherine to a sister who had withdrawn from the community.

"We may still hope to see each other, but when? You are aware that when one leaves the Community we no longer hold communication with her. You know our rules. At present, more than ever, fevor is renewed in the Community as in the time of Saint Vincent. If abuses have existed, now all is being reinstated." Significant words, revealing at the same time the humility of the Servant of God and the untiring activity of the Superior General.

In May 1845 the daughters of Charity had chosen as their Superioress Mother Mazin who became in virtue of her eminent capabilities and devotion to the Company, an intelligent and zealous colaborer of Father Etienne in the recently inaugurated work of reform. "From this epoch," writes one of the sisters, "we seemed to have returned to the golden days when

144

THE TWO FAMILIES OF SAINT VINCENT

Blessed Louise de Marillac, directed by Saint Vincent, laid the foundation of the Community. Under this twofold direction inspired solely by the tender charity of the Divine Master, the Daughters of Charity found happiness in obedience. Blind submission and prompt compliance to the wishes of Superiors reigned everywhere. What a beautiful spectacle the Mother House presented! Piety, recollection and union made it an abode of delights, and the serenity depicted on every countenance revealed the peace and joy of those who dwelt within."

But how to testify their gratitude by some fitting memorial, expressive of the appreciation of such boundless favors, now became the concern of Superiors. Toward the end of the year 1845 Divine Providence through the agency of Sister Catherine's director, appeared to furnish the means. Named Assistant to Father Etienne two years before, Father Aladel had received from the Baroness de Lupe the gift of a house near Dax in the diocese of Aire. This was to be converted into an establishment for the Priests of the Mission. It

was on November twenty-first, the feast of the Presentation of the Blessed Virgin, that the Sons of
Saint Vincent, who for years had conducted the
mission in the diocese of Landes as well as the
Pilgrimage of Our Lady of Buglose, amid unutterable joy took possession of the new foundation in
the very birthplace of their Holy Founder.

In his "History of the Establishment and Works
of the House of Our Lady of Pouy," Father
Truquet, the first Superior, writes: "The chapel
was blessed and the altar placed under the invocation of the Immaculate Conception, in return for
the signal favors granted the little Company
through her mediation during the last fifteen years."
The good Superior sets forth another noteworthy
incident which antedated Lourdes by ten years:
"Although this motive be of itself sufficient to
justify the choice of the Superior General and Father Aladel as to the title of the chapel, it is not
however the only motive. For might it not be in
the designs of Providence, that the dedication of
the chapel to the Immaculate Conception, should
give impulse to the inauguration of a pilgrimage

146

thither in honor of Our Lady?" Such were the aspirations of Fathers Etienne and Aladel.

But providence directed otherwise. For while Dax is only a short distance from Lourdes, still trains bearing thousands of Catholics to the feet of Mary Immaculate, speed by the Chapel of the Missionaries, on to the rocks of Massabielle. Thus Father Aladel, the initiator of the idea of a pilgrimage to Our Lady of Pouy, and his friend, Father Etienne, were destined by Providence to attract other multitudes to the statue of the most holy Virgin in Paris. It is, however, none other than the Supreme Pontiff, Pius IX, the Pope of the Immaculate Conception, who will determine conclusively the monument which connected with their names will be a perpetual memorial of the favors bestowed in 1830.

The day after his elevation to the Holy See, Pius IX wrote to Father Etienne: "As your illustrious Institute is now, by the grace of God, spread throughout the Catholic world, with so great profit to souls, it preëminently appeals to Us as an especial object of interest. We, therefore, earnestly

147

desire that you should be perfectly persuaded that nothing will be more agreeable to Us, nothing more conformable to our intentions, than to embrace every opportunity of enhancing the glory of your two families." This expression of good-will of the Holy Father, dated August 25, 1846, was realized the next year by the concession of a peculiar privilege, the establishment of a new association, which in the bosom of the two families of Saint Vincent de Paul, constitutes, as it were a third order—the Association of the Children of Mary.

CHAPTER VII

THE CHILDREN OF MARY

1847—1865

IT was on June 20, 1847 that Father Etienne, Superior General of the two families of Saint Vincent, already the recipient of divers faculties and privileges from the newly elected Pope, Pius IX, solicited of the Holy Father that of establishing in the schools conducted by the Daughters of Charity, a pious association under the title of "Most Holy Virgin Immaculate." He begged His Holiness that the new association be enriched with all the indulgences granted to the Congregation of the Most Holy Virgin, erected in Rome for the students of the Society of Jesus. The Sovereign Pontiff graciously granted the favor and signed the concession with his own hand. Such is the official and canonical act of the authorization of the Association of the Children of Mary.

But the origin of the association can in all truth be traced to the events of 1830, to Sister Catherine Labouré. In concluding her twofold narrative of the interview with which the Blessed Virgin favored her on the night of the eighteenth of July 1830, the Seer writes: "I recall that I one day said to Father Aladel, 'The Blessed Virgin asks of you another mission; she wishes you to establish an order of which you will be the founder and director. It is a confraternity of Children of Mary. Many graces, many indulgences will be granted to it and by it many feasts will be brought about.' "

The first mission entrusted to the director of Sister Catherine was that he have the Miraculous Medal struck and disseminated; the second, that he assist Father Etienne in the work of reviving the primitive spirit in the two families of Saint Vincent, and the third that, just referred to by the Seer.

He who was personally designated by the Blessed Virgin to organize the Sodality of the Children of Mary, was born May 4, 1800 in Cantal. At the time of the first apparitions to

150

THE CHILDREN OF MARY

Sister Catherine, Father John Mary Aladel was thirty years of age. His recognized piety and consummate prudence were in such repute that many sought counsel of him. In 1834 Jules Simon, at the time in attendance at the Normal School, laid his doubts on religious matters before the young priest. Writes the philosopher in his "Memoirs of Other Men": "He was what the gospel styles a fisher of men. He received me with gravity and kindness." Chosen assistant of the Congregation of the Mission at the age of thirty-five, Father Aladel, now in official position, was empowered to accomplish gradually the new mission assigned him by the Blessed Virgin.

In Côte d'Or not far from the birthplace of Sister Catherine Labouré we find traces of the Association of the Children of Mary. Thanks to records faithfully guarded by pious tradition, it is in our power to produce a brief sketch of the young girl selected by Father Aladel to be the first flower offered to the Immaculate Virgin.

This was Bénigne Hairon. Born at Baune in the diocese of Dijon in 1822, of an honorable

151

though reduced family, she became the first inmate of the orphanage conducted by the Daughters of Charity there. On December 8, 1838, at sixteen years of age she was chosen, as she loved to repeat, "the first of all the Children of Mary." Bénigne manifested an extraordinary devotion to the Blessed Virgin and never failed to recite daily the Little Office of the Immaculate Conception and the rosary. In the capacity of governess in the establishment, she assisted the Sisters and shared the common life of the children in work-room, refectory and dormitory. She began her day's labor habitually at four o'clock, on Communion days at three, and spent the greater part of her free time in the chapel. Of remarkable poise and equanimity, she seemed never disturbed, and though a victim of neuralgia, was never known to yield to impatience or complaint. Among the children her preference was always for the most wayward, the least prepossessing. Her great delicacy of conscience caused her to flee the merest shadow of sin. Unconcerned about the world of which she knew little, she observed an extreme

152

simplicity of manner, clinging to the costume of her native place, even to the muslin cap. It is alleged by the Sisters who saw her at work that in this saintly soul all the virtues were assembled and that her one aim in all she did was the good pleasure of God. A most painful sacrifice must needs crown a life so replete with virtue. In 1903 the Daughters of Charity were compelled to withdraw from Baune, and Bénigne, then eighty-one years of age, was obliged to seek refuge at the Hotel Dieu, whence, separated from those whom she cherished here below, after three years of patient suffering and edifying resignation, she went to her God.

The Association of the Children of Mary at Baune of which Bénigne Hairon was the eldest sister, was established February 2, 1840. By degrees other branches were formed: at Bordeaux, Saint Eulalie, March 19, 1840; Saint Flour in 1841; at Mainsat, Creuse in 1842; at Bazas, Gironde and at Albi in 1844; at Mans, Rennes, Aurillac and Aubusson in 1845.

On December 16, 1845 the first association of Paris was erected with Father Aladel as

153

director. Should the reader wish to become acquainted with one of the most touching phases
of the new confraternity, he need but sketch the
register of the Association of the Children of Mary
established in the Orphanage of L'Ile Saint Louis,
Paris. Herein are recorded the minutes of the
corporate meetings and a complete list of all the
associates with a brief history of each. Whence
too we gather information that of the eighteen
Children of Mary entered at the first reception,
seven were received into religious communities,
four having become Daughters of Charity.

The second and by far the more interesting
portion of the register, treats partly of edifying
remarks on the deceased members and partly of
private correspondence of the early associates and
contains also several letters of interest received
from various centres. This association of L'Ile
Saint Louis was, as it were, the little Mother
House of the rising confraternity. That sentiments
of cordial affection united the members is admirably attested by the appellation "Sisters, little

THE CHILDREN OF MARY

Sisters" mutually interchanged in this interesting correspondence.

In the environs of Picpus, near the Orphanage d'Enghien, where Sister Catherine continued to live in obscurity, was an extensive district, poor and populous, under the exclusive control of Protestant deaconesses. The necessity of establishing as a counterpoise to this influence, some works of Catholic charity was obvious to the Daughters of Charity of the House Enghien. Let us see the part that Heaven took in the new group of works that sprang into existence. We shall instance only one feature relative to the foundation of a school, a need considered by the sisters of paramount importance.

A sister of the Orphanage of Enghien, Jeanne Bergerault, in community Sister Vincent, while on an errand of mercy in behalf of a poor conscript whose departure plunged his family into utter misery, experienced as she crossed Rue de l'Université a passing strange sensation. An interior voice kept whispering to her "Madame de Narbonne, Madame de Narbonne." Amazed at the

repetition of a name wholly unknown to her, Sister
Vincent prayed the Divine Master for light. She
stopped and inquired whether the address of a
certain Lady Narbonne was known. Some one
replied in the affirmative, stating that the Sister was
at the very door of the Duchess.

Deciding on the spot to ask the favor of an audience, she was admitted and having interested the
Duchess in the conscript, received a thousand
francs to procure his ransom. During the next
few nights the same name continued to reverberate
in her mind. She seemed pressed to repeat her
visit to the benign lady and engage her interest
in the establishment of a Catholic school. To her
intense satisfaction Madame de Narbonne signalized
her approval of the scheme by agreeing to rent a
house adjoining the Orphanage to accommodate
the children. It is difficult to conceive the joy of
the Sisters of Enghien when a few days later the
school was in readiness. Other works quickly followed, namely, an asylum, a workroom for both
these living in the house and for outsiders, and a
place of aid for young girls.

THE CHILDREN OF MARY

As soon as these works were inaugurated, Father Aladel sought to establish there an Association of the Children of Mary. The first assembly was held November 21, 1851, Feast of the Presentation of the Blessed Virgin. The minutes of the proceedings read as follows: "For some time having learned of the Association of the Children of Mary, we longed to be sharers of the great privilege but were checked by an obstacle that seemed insurmountable. We are too young, we would sadly say one to another, and the Father Director would not consent to receive us; just now we cannot hope to be ranked with those privileged ones whose hearts are consecrated to the Queen of Virgins. . . . .

"Yet, our heartfelt desire had been heard by the motherly love of the august Virgin. One of her devoted servants whose zeal and charity to gain hearts to her love knew no bounds, was now sent to us. This visitor, who spoke to us of the association, was none other than Father Aladel, the Director of the Daughters of Charity. A ray of hope had dawned! On the Feast of the Presen-

tation this hope was fulfilled through the same
Father Aladel and this in the presence of our good
Mother and beloved teachers as well as of several
Sisters of the Community." It is safe to say that
Sister Catherine was of the number, participating
in the joy of her sisters, while dissembling her own.

"The altar of the Blessed Virgin was adorned
with its richest ornaments. The children in holi-
day attire were on one side of the chapel, and
the girls of the workroom on the other. After
an exhortation calculated to excite our piety,
Father Aladel proceeded to receive the aspir-
ants. One of them in the name of all recited
the customary act of consecration. We received
from the hand of the Director the green ribbon,
pledge of our hope, and the precious medal attached thereto. With this ceremony we imagined
the feast had ended when we heard the Director
ask if there were not some who might at once be
admitted as Children of Mary. Our good Mother
designated three, Esther, Antoinette and Zoé. To
our great astonishment we saw the Director advance toward the altar. Then he bade the three

158

children drew near. As we knelt before him he placed around our necks the precious medal, powerful weapon to repulse the demon. He next gave us the Manual wherein were detailed our duties. Benediction of the Blessed Sacrament crowned this memorable feast." How similar the order of exercises to that in vogue today at the reception of the Children of Mary!

As early as 1850 the Superior General was empowered by the Holy See to enroll in the Family of Mary Immaculate the children and young men educated in the houses of the Priests of the Mission or confided to the care of the Daughters of Charity. What a note of enthusiastic gratitude we detect in the description of the reception of these youthful workers of Reuilly into the Sodality of Children of Mary! We insert it in its entirety.

"God be praised because of the noble work that has developed among us! Praise and glory to the Mother of our Savior who has deigned to open the door of the association to her other children! May this monument erected to the omnipotent and

all-merciful God on the ruins of sin and death,
prove our gratitude to the Immaculate by whose
potent protection we have been rescued from evils
to which we should most certainly have fallen
victims.

"Never was there witnessed a spectacle more
touching and tender than that of our blessed
reunion. Gathered around the radiantly beautiful
altar we awaited in profound recollection the hour
of the august ceremony,—that hour which was to
witness our protestations of fidelity to the Most
Holy Virgin. At last the longed-for moment
arrived. What joy, what emotion was depicted on
the countenance of each of us! The ministers
of the Lord advanced to the altar. The Superior
General made a brief but soul-stirring address,
demonstrating that honorable service can be rendered to society even in the humble walks of life.
'A man' said he 'is not ennobled by position or
rank, on the contrary it is the man who ennobles
his condition.' Then in proof of what he said he
instanced the deplorable weakness of Eve and its
attendant depth of humiliation, affecting not herself

alone but all posterity. In contrast he portrayed the exalted virtues and heroic actions of Mary as regaining that which had been lost by the sin of our first mother. Finally, he exhorted us to honor by the tenor of our conduct the association which we were about to enter, the only way we might render ourselves worthy of the beautiful title 'Children of Mary.' Then followed the reception. The whole ceremony was concluded by the Benediction of the Blessed Sacrament. The singing was rendered by some of the members who acquitted themselves with an ardor indicating that they joyed in their privilege of praising God and His Immaculate Mother."

A few months later Father Aladel, the founder and director of the Children of Mary, terminated his earthly career. He died April 25, 1865, the thirty-fifth anniversary of the Translation of the Relics of Saint Vincent de Paul. It is believed that the director of Sister Catherine, emulating the heroic action of the young Father Dufour in favor of Saint Vincent, offered his life to obtain the cure of Father Etienne then dangeriously ill at Dax. Beautiful act which sheds a new glory about the memory of the faithful servant of Mary. He whose lips had so often proclaimed Mary's praises, this emulator of the beloved Saint John, this other Saint Bernard, was now still in death. No longer might he propose to the Children of Mary, the Apostle of virginity and charity as their model by excellence, and as the first among the adopted sons of Mary. No longer might he be heard invoking in loving epithets Mary Immaculate, endeavoring to enkindle in youthful hearts the flame of love that glowed so brightly in his own.

But how was Sister Catherine affected by the death of her director? From an eye-witness in attendance at the funeral obsequies of Father Aladel, we learn that she alone amid the universal sorrowing was radiant with joy. Or in his own words: "I was astonished on beholding the joyful expression of her countenance. I could not comprehend it." How easy of solution today! What else but a favorable judgment could be accorded the humble priest who as God's deputy had so gloriously achieved the threefold mission of disseminating the Miraculous Medal, of assisting in the reformation of the two families of Saint Vincent de Paul, and of establishing and directing the Association of the Children of Mary? And who appreciated this more than Sister Catherine? No, the Servant of God was not insensible to the loss. Her spirit of faith showed her that the separation was but temporary. In a few short years she too, after having presented to the angels and to her companions the ideal type of a Daughter of Charity, would take her heavenward flight.

CHAPTER VIII

A TRUE DAUGHTER OF CHARITY

IN one of his celebrated conferences Saint Vincent de Paul has sketched the portrait of a true Daughter of Charity. Says the Saint, "the virtues that should characterize the servant of the sick poor are those of the good village girl. The first subjects who entered the Company were village girls. Moreover, it was by means of these virtues that the Patroness of Paris, the illustrious Saint Genevieve, attained her high degree of sanctity."

How closely Sister Catherine Labouré, who during the last ten years of her mortal life, presented to the gaze of all an accomplished model of an ideal Daughter of Charity, resembled Saint Genevieve! The remarks of those who between 1866 and 1876 came in contact with our Blessed Sister, bear witness to the fact that she possessed in the highest degree the virtues of simplicity,

164

humility, sobriety, modesty, poverty and obedience, as our holy Founder understood them.

In the first place "true village girls are extremely simple." They go straight to God in all things for such is the significance of simplicity. By this spirit was the Servant of God actuated in her relations with Him, in her behavior toward her companions and in her intercourse with her family. Indeed simplicity directed all the events of her life. There was no self-seeking in the devotions of Sister Catherine Labouré. Our Lord and the Blessed Virgin—around these two names her whole interior life centered. The Sacred Heart of Jesus, and the Immaculate Heart of Mary so intimately united with that of her divine Son, sufficed to nurture the piety and satisfy the ardor of her contemplative soul.

During morning prayer which began at half-past four, Sister Catherine remained kneeling, always very erect, unsupported save by the tips of her fingers which rested lightly on the priedieu. Once asked how to make meditation, she replied: "It is easy. When I go to the chapel, I place myself in the presence of God and say to Him 'Dear Lord, here I am; give unto me according to Thy pleasure.' Should He favor me, I am well pleased and thank Him, but if I have received nothing, still I thank Him, recognizing that I deserve nothing. I speak freely to Him as thoughts present. I relate my trials and my joys and then I listen. For in dealing with God we must first speak and then attend to His answer. It always comes when we draw near in simplicity and confidence."

Her preparation for Holy Communion began the day before its reception. To the young Sisters whom she desired to adopt this practice, she would say: "Come, little ones, you must offer some sacrifice to God in preparation for your Communion of tomorrow." On her return from the Holy Table it was visible to all how profoundly absorbed she was in the presence of her King. During the day, if visited by trial, especially when a humiliation presented, she would go to the chapel, remain a few moments in converse with her God, then resume her occupation, her peaceful and amiable countenance revealing the serenity of

Ste CATHERINE LABOURÉ

She knew how to
keep the secret
of her King
but above all the
secret of
her Queen.

Pius XI

her soul. To a Sister who had received a reprimand she once said: "My dear Sister, if you have anything to say, go to the foot of the altar. Tell it to our Lord; He will not divulge it. And you will derive strength to bear up under the trial."

During her long life at the House of Enghien Sister Catherine was variously employed, but toward the end of her career she was charged with the office of portress. Quietly seated in her little room she labored under the eye of God alone. How the old Sisters would seek her out to recite with her the chaplet! "She says it so well," they would say, "with such attention and unction, pronouncing each word without hurry. The very tone of her voice invites to devotion." And her last Sister Servant relates: "When the Sisters said the rosary in common, we were always impressed by the grave and devout accent with which our dear companion pronounced the words of the angelical salutation. Deeply penetrated with sentiments of religious respect and piety, this soul otherwise so humble and reserved, could not refrain from censuring the levity and inattention that un-

167

fortunately accompany the repetition of this admirable and efficacious prayer."

At the Hospital of Enghien Sister Catherine acquitted herself of her charge, the care of the old men, in a spirit of faith and supernatural simplicity. Interrogated as to why she did not administer a reprimand to one of her patients who was unreasonable in his demands, she replied, "I see our Lord in him."

"What a wicked old fellow N. is!" said another.

"Ah well! pray for him," was her simple rejoinder.

And how her concern for the spiritual interests of her patients redoubled as death drew near! On the testimony of Sister Dufès we assert that during the sixteen years they lived together at the hospital, no person died without being reconciled with his God.

Between the Hospital of Enghien and the House of Reuilly, both of which were under the administration of the same superioress, there was a

168

garden. It was noticed that whenever the requirements of her office obliged Sister Catherine to
cross this, she always paused before a statue of the
Virgin. With hands joined and eyes uplifted she
appeared as one transfigured. More than once the
Children of Mary and the postulants of the House
of Reuilly concealed themselves behind the bushes
to get a glimpse of the Seer thus absorbed in silent
contemplation. It was while praying before the
same statue that she was surprised by a companion
one day before morning prayer.

But what shall we say of her evening meditation?
In the chapel before the tabernacle the Servant of
God, in full view of her Sisters, her eyes riveted
on the statue of the Blessed Virgin, knelt in very
ecstasy. And yet this favored soul notwithstanding her spirit of prayer and her uninterrupted contact with God and things divine, would accuse
herself of having failed in her acts of the presence
of God. In Him she lived and Him she saw in
each of her companions. "It sometimes happened"
said a Sister of Enghien, "that having witnessed
some trying circumstance of which she was the

victim, I expressed my displeasure but she merely answered in her calm, gentle way: "No matter, it is for the good God." Again to those who offered sympathy, she would say: "We should in all things recognize the will of God."

In her relations with her family our Blessed Sister was kind and cordial but ever becomingly reserved. She loved her own in God. She could say with Saint Vincent de Paul: "Think you that I do not love my relatives? I have for them all the tenderness one could have for one's own..... yet I must act according to the inspirations of grace, not the promptings of nature." Aunt Zoé as she was familiarly called by her own, interested herself principally in their spiritual welfare and in the salvation of their souls.

One of her brothers having abandoned the practice of his religion, Sister Catherine urged the family to exercise a vigilant care over him lest falling dangerously ill he might be deprived in death of the solace of the Last Sacraments. Another brother, James, being at the point of death, was visited by the Servant of God, who learning that he had received the Sacraments, placed about his neck a Miraculous Medal and withdrew.

But it was for her nephew Philip that she cherished an especial affection, Philip, who had just begun his studies with the curé of the little village of Viserny, not far from Fain-les-Moutiers in Cote d' Or. Sister Catherine acquainted herself directly and indirectly with his dispositions toward what she divined was an incipient attraction for the priesthood. She found that he really entertained such a desire and thereupon called him to Paris that she herself, with the authorization of Superiors, might conduct him to the College of Montdidier.

Toward the end of his secondary studies the young man visited his aunt at the Hospital of Enghien. After asking if he still persevered in his intention, she added: "Should you desire to join the Congregation, these gentlemen will receive you." Then said the Servant of God, a slight smile on her lips:

"You may soon be named Superior. . . . . You may travel; see countries; go on mission; even

to China, as did the Blessed Perboyre." In her
hand she held a small wooden reliquary containing a fragment of the clothing once worn by the
venerable martyr. She then concluded: "Yes,
and you may also return from distant shores."

And from the nephew we have the statement:
"All these sayings I regarded as mere surmises on
the part of Sister Catherine to ascertain what I, a
young man of seventeen, thought about my future.
Abruptly closing the conversation, I remarked,
'Time will tell.'"

Did her nephew see the fulfillment of that conversation of his "virtuous aunt" as she was styled
by Father Chinchon, Director of the Novitiate of
the Congregation and Sister Catherine's confessor?

Here are the facts. This nephew entered the
Congregation at Saint Lazare. When quite young
he was appointed Superior of the Seminary of
Saint Pons in the south of France. Thence he
was sent to the East where for many years he
filled the position of Procurator and Visitor of the
Chinese missions. Later recalled to France, he

A TRUE DAUGHTER OF CHARITY

was in 1899 named Assistant of the Congregation of the Mission and Director of the Daughters of Charity at the very time when the Canonical Inquiry concerning the life and virtues of Sister Catherine was in progress.

The mother of Father M., none other than the little "Tonine" of Fain-les-Moutiers, also enjoyed the comforting presence of the Servant of God at her deathbed, In her later years she made Paris her home. Taking a retrospect of her life one day, she remarked to her sister Zoé: "Had I known what would happen to me, I would have become a religious such as you."

"Each one according to her vocation," replied Sister Catherine. "Had such been the case you would not have enjoyed the privilege of giving one of your sons to God."

It was January 18, 1874. Marie Antoinette had been confined to her bed for several months. Having fallen into a comatose condition, she spoke rarely and apparently knew no one. About one o'clock in the afternoon Sister Catherine

called to see her sister and requested her niece
Madame D. with her two daughters to withdraw.
Our Blessed Sister remained alone for an hour
with the sick woman.   What had transpired in
that interval?   Presently the door of the chamber
opened and Sister Catherine appeared.

"Now" she said quietly, "go to your mother."
Marie Antoinette was fully awake and with entire composure gave her last advices to her daughter and grandchildren.   Shortly after this, she
lapsed into unconsciousness and on January
twentieth at four in the morning gently expired.
While her sister was soaring to Heaven there to
enjoy the presence of God without shadow of
change, our Blessed Sister continued to see Him
here below in all the occurrences of life.

Just as surely as the revolving year brought
with it the great feasts of Our Lady, Sister Catherine was visited by some keen suffering which increased with her advanced age.   What gratitude
filled her bosom as she joyfully accepted what she
termed these providential favors!   On the occasion
of one Feast of the Immaculate Conception she

174

with other Sisters spent the day at Rue du Bac.
That evening when entering the omnibus Sister
Catherine slipped and broke her wrist. She said
nothing of the accident nor did any one perceive
it at the time. Later Sister Dufès noticing her
hand enveloped in a handkerchief, asked what
had happened.

"Ah! my Sister, I am holding my bouquet,"
answered the Servant of God. "Every year the
Blessed Virgin sends me some such present."

With the same supernatural tranquillity, with the
same remarkable simplicity she accepted the dis-
tressing and alarming events of the war of the
Commune 1870—1871. She would often repeat:
"We must pray that God may shorten the evil
days." One day in April 1871 during recreation
the Servant of God said to her Superioress: "I
had a strange dream last night. The Blessed
Virgin came to the community room. You were
not present. She then went to your office and not
finding you, seated herself at your desk and said to
me: 'Since Sister Dufès is not here, tell her for
me that she can leave with safety. I shall take

175

possession of the house and safeguard it. She will go south with Sister Claire but will return by the thirty-first of May.' "

This occurred about the time of the proclamation of the Commune. Next day upon meeting her Superioress Sister Catherine said to her:

"My Sister, do not pay much attention to what I told you."

"My dear Sister Catherine," replied the other, "I have not given it a thought."

The fact that these predictions were verified to the letter seems to indicate that there was here question of more than a dream. For had not the Blessed Virgin said after the three great apparitions of 1830?

"My child, you will not see me henceforth, but you will hear my voice in your meditations."

But in what manner were they verified? It was Good Friday, April 7, 1871. A band of communists in quest of two gendarmes whom they intended to shoot, had forced an entrance into the house of Sister Dufès which had been transformed into an ambulance. They withdrew, however, without having secured their prey. Two days later their chief came to Providence Sainte Marie and demanded of the Superioress the surrender of the two men.

"Never," exclaimed Sister Dufès.

Swords were raised over her and an attempt was made to seize her by the arm.

"Do not touch me," she cried with great force and dignity.

She was then ordered to the prison of Saint Lazare where some religious and two Daughters of Charity were already incarcerated. The companions of Sister Dufès, forty strong, surrounded their Superioress, declaring that they would follow her. The long file of cornettes had advanced to the threshold when the wretch who had given the order reconsidered the matter and released the Sisters, saying to those about him:

"What shall I do with these affrighted swallows?"

"You will hear from me tomorrow," he added and was gone.

On the morrow Sister Dufès personally threatened by an order of arrest, managed to escape and was conveyed by carriage to Versailles. Behold the first part of Sister Catherine's dream realized. Her Superioress was in safety.

After a few days of untold anxiety, without adverting to the words of our Blessed Sister, Sister Dufès said to one of her companions about to set out for Paris to seek information:

"Send me Sister Claire. If I must leave the hospital for a while, we shall go south." Thus what had been forseen by Sister Catherine actually came to pass. The Superioress of Enghien accompanied by Sister Claire D'Aragon sought safety in the House of Saint Michel, Toulouse.

Meanwhile the Servant of God, faithful to her duty as portress, lost no opportunity of distributing the medal among the soldiers then quartered in the hospital. One of the sisters relates that all the soldiers stationed at Enghien came to her saying:

A TRUE DAUGHTER OF CHARITY

"We are looking for the venerable Sister who has given medals to our comrades. They showed them to us. Now it is our turn to get them."

"But you," said the Sister, "poor fellows, have neither faith nor religion. What good will medals do you?"

"True, Sister, we have very little faith, but we believe in that medal. It has protected others; it will also protect us. Should we be under fire it will help us to die like brave men."

And Sister Catherine delighted in satisfying as many as presented themselves. Even the soldiers on guard relieved by their comrades, came to the hospital to secure a medal.

As a measure of prudence the Sisters departed from the hospital on the thirtieth of April. On the eve of their departure Sister Catherine was summoned to appear before an improvised tribunal installed in the community room of Providence Saint Marie. Conducted thither by two soldiers she was subjected to a formal though inconsequential inquiry. Before leaving the premises Sister

BLESSED CATHERINE LABOURÉ

Catherine with one of her sisters repaired to the garden and gazing at the favorite statue of her heavenly Mother, besought Mary Immaculate to reassemble all the sisters in their beloved mission to celebrate the close of her own beautiful month.

That evening at six o'clock the sisters left the hospital. The bags containing the personal effects were subjected to inspection and the Servant of God had the mortification of seeing the contents of hers contemptuously scattered by the communist. Silently enduring this mockery she gathered her poor belongings and with her companions entered the omnibus. On the way from the Faubourg Saint Antoine to the Barrière du Thröne, the Daughters of the charitable Vincent de Paul could hear the wretched mothers urging their very babes in arms to utter injurious words and sinster threats against them.

Having received a cordial welcome from Sister Rendier at Saint Denis, Sister Catherine was not slow to perceive that hospitality was extended to her personally since the administration allowed this privilege to but one Sister.

A TRUE DAUGHTER OF CHARITY

"I do not wish to remain here alone," said Sister Catherine to her companion. "I might die. At that moment I want one of my companions with me. If you consent, we shall go together to Balainviliers, to Sister Mattavant who has offered me a home. I beg of you not to leave me."

From Seine-et-Oise the Servant of God wrote a long letter to her Superioress but unfortunately it has not been preserved. Therein she renewed the assurance that the end of May would see them all together again at the House of Reuilly.

On May eighth it was announced that a detachment of the "Avengers of the Republic" had perpetrated infamous sacrileges at the Church of Our Lady of Victory.

"See," said Sister Catherine to her companion, "they have dared touch Our Lady. Well, this act will prove their downfall. They will go no futher."

And so it happened. On Sunday May twenty-first the troops of Versailles broke through the siege works of Paris and reached the capital by way of Auteuil and other posts. The regular army had triumphed over the insurrectionists.

On May thirtieth Sister Dufès returning from Toulouse, betook herself to Balainvilliers in search of Sister Catherine and her companion. The next day Wednesday, May thirty-first, witnessed the Daughters of Charity reinstated in the Houses of Enghien and Reuilly which were protected from pillage through the efforts of the Children of Mary. At the five o'clock Mass on that morning Sister Eugénie Mauche, Superioress of the Daughters of Charity from 1910 to 1912, pronounced her First Holy Vows.

"Did I not tell you, my good Mother, that I would come back and crown you on the thirty-first of May?" exclaimed Sister Catherine, as she replaced on the brow of the statue of the Blessed Virgin the crown she had taken with her at her departure. Amid such disastrous events the Servant of God preserved an unalterable peace of soul, simplicity of faith and above all confidence in God.

If we have dwelt at length on the first of the

virtues that should distinguish a Daughter of Charity, it is that the reader may duly appreciate the virtue of simplicity which was the very life of Sister Catherine Labouré. But Saint Vincent is not satisfied that his Daughters emulate merely the simplicity of these good village girls. "The humility of these good people," continues the Saint, "precludes all ambition. They are perfectly content with what God gives them. Neither do they desire greater riches than they possess." Such was our Blessed Sister.

On one occasion two young ladies who had completed their postulatum and were about to leave the House of Reuilly for Rue du Bac, accosted Sister Catherine with:

"Tomorrow, Sister, we leave for the Seminary. Tell us something about the Blessed Virgin." This request they made in the hope of eliciting from our Blessed Sister some observations on the Chapel of the Apparitions, for at the time Sister Catherine was under suspicion as the Seer of Rue du Bac.

"Ah! my dear young ladies," said the Sister, "make a good use of your seminary, and cherish a special devotion to our Blessed Mother."

On another occasion one of the Sisters of the House of Enghien, was entertaining a very dear friend. Chancing to meet Sister Catherine at the door, she whispered to her visitor:

"There is the Sister of the apparitions of 1830."

"My dear Sister," exclaimed the young lady, advancing toward Sister Catherine, "how charmed I am to meet the one so highly favored by the vision of the Miraculous Medal!"

A look of utter astonishment was Sister Catherine's only reply. By this time the Sister conscious of her imprudence vainly endeavored to repair her blunder by saying in a low voice: "The Sister wishes to remain unknown." That evening the Superioress of Enghien having heard what had occurred, bade her young companion ask pardon of Sister Catherine for the indiscretion. She did so in these terms;

"My Sister, I was told in the Seminary that the

184

A TRUE DAUGHTER OF CHARITY

Blessed Virgin appeared to the Sister in charge of the chicken yard at Enghien and I believe it."

"But, my little one," graciously replied our Sister, "know that it is very imprudent thus to speak at random."

Once during recreation a companion of Sister Catherine remarked in her presence: "Very probably the Sisters who had been favored by the visions of the Miraculous Medal and the Scapular of the Passion, were to be found among Superiors."

"No, no," replied the Servant of God, "such souls should lead a hidden life."

"Perhaps both are dead," ventured the Sister.

"Who knows?" replied Sister Catherine, "Who can tell that?"

The last time our Blessed Sister spoke to Sister Dufès of the apparitions of 1830, the latter congratulated her on the favors she received from the Most Holy Virgin.

"I favored! my good Sister," exclaimed Sister Catherine. "I was only an instrument. It was not

on my account that the Blessed Virgin appeared.
I knew nothing, not even how to write. I am indebted to the Community for whatever I know.
That is why the Blessed Virgin selected me, lest
any one should doubt."

And her spirit of mortification! "Good village
girls observe great sobriety in eating and drinking.
The greater number are content with bread and
soup though they live a laborious life. It is thus
you should act," said our Blessed Father speaking
to his first Daughters, "if you wish to be true
Daughters of Charity."

How Sister Catherine practiced this virtue the
following instance from the pen of her Superioress
will illustrate: "She served us at table and invari-
ably reserved for herself whatever was least pala-
table. 'This is for the Superior,' she would say
to the young Sister charged with distributing the
food in the refectory. 'This for the sick; these
for the Community.' And when all had been
served she would add: 'And this for me, if you
please.'"

A TRUE DAUGHTER OF CHARITY

In November 1876, Sister Elizabeth was placed on duty in the kitchen. The Servant of God was exceedingly interested in her, instructed her in regard to the requirements of her office, the preparation of the food, the proper quantity to be served each, etc., etc.

"During her last illness," states Sister Elizabeth, "I tried to find what she preferred but her invariable reply was:

"Whatever you wish, Sister."

When I pressed her to tell me, she would say:

"An egg will do, thank you." So totally indifferent was she to all that concerned the body.

In speaking to his Daughters Saint Vincent de Paul who exacted of them no ordinary degree of virtue, failed not to aid them in its attainment. He says: "These good village girls, those at least who resemble the great Saint Genevieve, possess a remarkable purity. You should never listen to anything that would be detrimental to the purity that should distinguish you. Blessed be God who has until now preserved you from all danger!"

BLESSED CATHERINE LABOURE

The very presence of Sister Catherine betokened her virginal purity. Her eyes habitually lowered could not conceal entirely the crystal clearness of her glance, the perfect purity of her heart. Among the patients in the Hospital of Enghien there were some whose manners left much to be desired, yet not one ever dared, in the presence of Sister Catherine, infringe in the slightest degree the rules of strict reserve. And her Superioress testified that to the Servant of God was given the supernatural power of discerning such as were wanting in this virtue which shone in herself with such refulgence.

And her nieces, the grandchildren of Marie Antoinette, declared: 'We took so much pleasure in going to wish Sister Catherine a 'Happy Feast.' On such occasions we always presented her with a bouquet of white flowers with orange blossoms in the centre." This bouquet was at once carried to the chapel, a fit offering in honor of the glory of Mary conceived without sin, while at the same time it symbolized the innocence of her privileged child.

If purity should be the chief ornament of the true Daughter of Charity, poverty should be her

188

sole treasure. "As a good village girl, Saint Genevieve loved poverty," said Saint Vincent to our first Sisters. "Therefore, you too should esteem and love the practice of this virtue. Mark, I use the word *practice*. It would indeed mean little merely to entertain an esteem for this virtue."

Sister Catherine Labouré's love of poverty was practical. "She would urge us," says a young Sister, "to take care of whatever was in our keeping. She would wear a habit, patched and darned yet always clean, until it reached the impossibility of service. Equally solicitous was she about the clothing of the old men under her care. In her little office as portress there were no fancy articles to be found. A statue of the Blessed Virgin of little artistic value and a crucifix were its only adornment."

"At her death," writes another, "we found nothing belonging to her. Many of us would have been so happy to secure some little souvenir but there was nothing available save a few turns of wire used in chaining beads."

BLESSED CATHERINE LABOURÉ

The last and the principal virtue which the Daughters of Charity ought to imitate in these good village girls is that of holy obedience. According to Saint Vincent "this virtue must be practiced without murmuring. That the will of God is made known by the order of obedience should be your firm conviction. Therefore you should allow yourself to be guided by divine Providence as a horse is guided by its rider."

It was not difficult to detect that Sister Catherine's one aim was to accomplish the orders of obedience. Kitchen, laundry, sick-ward, she welcomed in turn as if each were an office of distinction. On her very last feast day on earth, she was found by a Sister who came with a number of children to greet her, busily cleansing the hospital vessels.

"See, my children," she said, "I am doing the work of a Daughter of Charity. Such works are our pearls. We must jealously guard them lest others deprive us of our honors."

Upon meeting Sister Catherine for the first time a Sister struck with the dignified bearing of the

BLESSED CATHERINE IN ADVANCED AGE

A TRUE DAUGHTER OF CHARITY

Servant of God, and believing that she was fitted for a more honorable employment, ventured to ask her if she did not find her duty monotonous and wearisome.

"My Sister," she replied, "one is never wearied doing the will of God."

During the siege of Paris, her nephew, by this time elevated to the priesthood, called on his aunt.

"I found her," he says, "at the post of portress. Her conversation was more than usually familiar. At first she spoke of her youth at Fain-les-Moutiers. Then passing to Community experiences related that on a certain occasion, the Superioress of the Daughters of Charity, Mother Devos, sent for her and intimated her intention of appointing her Sister Servant or Superioress.

" 'O my good Mother,' exclaimed the Servant of God, 'you know full well that I am not suited for such an office.' And she added, 'They sent me back to Reuilly.' Her tone of voice seemed to imply, 'And they did well.' "

The honor of superiority which our Blessed

Sister disclaimed for herself, she revered in those appointed by legitimate authority.

"Touch not Superiors; their trust is sacred," she would say. "My little ones, do not murmur. Do not find fault with the orders of Superiors because they represent God."

One of her companions affirms: "I never heard her contradict or discuss a given order." If by chance she were asked,

"My Sister, what are you doing?"

"Sister Superior has directed it thus," she would say simply.

Another testifies: "Sister Catherine was very exact. She never commented on the requirements of Superiors. If told to do something more or less repugnant to her views, her usually pale countenance would flush but she remained silent and immediately acquiesced."

For many years the direction of the House of Enghien was virtually confided to Sister Catherine Labouré. In 1874 the authority with which the Servant of God had been invested was transferred

A TRUE DAUGHTER OF CHARITY

to a young Sister with the title of Assistant. Our Blessed Sister hastened to assure the Superioress of both houses of her submission saying:

"My dear Sister, do not grieve. Superiors have spoken. That suffices. We shall receive Sister Angélique as one sent by God and shall pay her the same obedience we are happy to render you." And she kept her word.

During the period of forty-six years spent at Enghien Sister Catherine had been under the administration of six Superioresses, namely, Sister Savard, Mother Montcellet, Mother Mazin, Sister Rendier, Sister Gaize and Sister Dufès. The last mentioned renders this testimony to the remarkable obedience of our Blessed Sister:

"Sister Catherine was distinguished by the faithful observance of our Holy Rules and Constitutions. During the sixteen years we lived together I do not remember to have known her ever to infringe them. She was in all things a light of edification to the Community. She would say, 'Mother has requested it.' 'Father has so decided.' 'Sister Superior wishes it. That suffices.' "

It seems but fitting to conclude this chapter on the virtues of Sister Catherine by quoting the words of Saint Vincent de Paul:

"Know, my dear Sisters, I have never spoken anything of greater importance than the words I have just uttered. I repeat. You should both corporally and spiritually comport yourselves as do good village girls who are bright examples of the virtues of simplicity, humility, sobriety, modesty, poverty and obedience." With Saint Vincent we would form the same wish. Let us add thereto another: "May they also resemble Sister Catherine in her holy and happy death."

CHAPTER IX

HER DEATH

DECEMBER 31, 1876

FROM the beginning of the year 1876 Sister Catherine had foretold her death. As the various feast days of Church and Community came round, she would say: "This is the last time I shall see this feast." Were doubt expressed as to the truth of this prophecy, she always added: "Of a truth, I shall not see 1877."

She expressed deep regret because the devotion to the Immaculate Conception had lost somewhat in that fervor and zeal for extension which had distinguished it immediately after the year 1830 and during the life time of Father Aladel. She knew full well that the first director of her conscience, carried off by an untimely death, had not been able to realize all the circumstances of the Manifestation of the Virgin Immaculate of November twenty-seventh. Believing herself on the verge of eternity she felt interiorly urged to communicate to her present confessor certain details which she believed buried with Father Aladel.

It was late May or early June 1876. Father Chinchon, Director of the Intern Seminary of the Congregation of the Mission, had for some time been the confessor of the Sisters of Enghien and Reuilly. Although he no longer served in that capacity, still it was to him that Sister Catherine desired to confide her last secrets and misgivings. She who rarely left the house, repaired, with the permission of her Superioress, to Rue de Sèvres, to Father Boré, Superior General of the Lazarists and of the Daughters of Charity, whose authorization to continue to address herself to Father Chinchon, she sought. The Superior unacquainted even with the motive, refused her request.

Sister Catherine returned home humbly submissive, though deeply grieved. Immediately seeking her Superioress, unable to restrain her tears, she said: "My dear Sister, I feel that my days are numbered. Since I am not permitted to confer

with my confessor, I shall address myself to you—
you know on what subject."

"My dear Sister Catherine," answered Sister
Dufès, who had received from Father Etienne
some intimation of the events of 1830, "it is true
that I have known that you received the Miraculous Medal from our Immaculate Mother, though
I have discreetly refrained from speaking of it to
you."

"Well, my Sister," interrupted Sister Catherine,
who had by this time recovered fron her emotion
and was mistress of herself, "tomorrow during my
meditation I shall consult the Blessed Virgin. If
she permits me to speak to you, I shall send for
you at ten o'clock. You will meet me in the
parlor at Enghien where we shall not be disturbed."

That evening the Superioress, mentioning the
incident to her Assistant, added: "Imagine my
anxiety while awaiting tomorrow morning." The
next day a little before ten Sister Catherine sent
for the Superioress who made no delay in crossing
the garden and there in the parlor of the Hospital

197

of Enghien the interview commenced. It consumed two hours and terminated just as the midday bell sounded the Angelus.

But what secret did the Seer confide to her Superioress?

"During the memorable interview," writes Sister Dufès, "when Sister Catherine gave me her confidence, she stated that the Blessed Virgin had appeared to her holding a globe in her hands. She then saw this divine Mother, her lips moving in prayer, offer the globe to her Son. Sister Catherine thereby understood that she was praying for the world."

"Here I interrupted her with 'There has never been mention of this globe in the hands of the Blessed Mother. If you speak of this it will be said that you have lost your mind.'

"It would not be the first time that I have been treated as insane," she replied, "yet even to my last sigh I shall maintain that the Blessed Virgin appeared to me holding in her hands a globe, representing the world."

HER DEATH

"What," I asked, "did the Blessed Virgin say when she offered the globe?"

"Ah! my Sister," said Sister Catherine, "I did not hear but I understood that she was praying for the whole world?"

"Well, afterwards what became of the globe offered by the Blessed Virgin?"

"Ah! my Sister, I do not know." Here Sister Catherine made a gesture extending her hands and then continued.

"I now saw only the rays that fell on the globe on which she stood, especially on a point marked France. The Blessed Virgin's hands were extended."

"But," I replied, "you will discredit the medal by speaking of the globe."

"No, no, my Sister, this does not concern the medal. A statue should be made of the Virgin holding the globe and an altar erected on the spot of the apparition. I should not like to appear before the Blessed Virgin ere this design be accomplished."

In confirmation of the truth of her words Sister Catherine mentioned two Sisters distinguished both for their virtue and for the intimate relations they had enjoyed with Father Aladel, Sister Pineau, sacristan at Rue du Bac and Sister Marie Grand de Boulogne, formerly Secretary at the Mother House under Father Aladel.

Sister Dufès declared that her admiration as she listened to the humble Sister relating so simply and with such perfect ease, the favors received from the Immaculate Mary, knew no bounds. "Could this truly be the same Sister Catherine habitually so silent and seemingly so deficient in expressing her thoughts?" she asked herself. "More than once" wrote the Superioress, "I felt like throwing myself on my knees before the favored one to crave pardon for not having appreciated her worth."

To place herself in immediate communication with the two Sisters designated by Sister Catherine now became an obligation on the part of Sister Dufès. Her letter to Sister Grand, Superioress of the Hospital at Riom, brought the following reply:

HER DEATH

"Yes, my good Sister Dufès, our loving Queen did appear with the globe of the world in her virginal hands. She held it close to her merciful heart contemplating it with ineffable tenderness. I also have a sketch designed many years ago representing her in this attitude, though I know not whether I can now find it. The venerated Father Aladel probably at the request of the Sister intended to preserve the memorable souvenir by having a representation made of this phase of the apparition. Yet this second attitude detracts nothing from the first, for the Most Holy Virgin, I believe, assumed the same position in both. Her arms were extended and rays of light fell upon the world which they deluged with the waves of her mercy, bestowing on all, especially on France, the gifts of predilection.

"It appears that at the moment the august Mother pressed the globe of the world to her pure heart, light from diamonds, carbuncles and other precious stones radiated from her maternal hands and covered our miserable earth enriching it with the gifts of her mercy and liberality. Again when she unfolded her arms waves of benediction and love flooded the world. Dear Sister Dufès, how I love to dwell on such sweet remembrances!

"It is to be regretted that our venerated Father Aladel failed to leave in writing the various details which he was not permitted to divulge during the life time of the Sister. 'Were I to do so,' said he, 'the favored one would be immediately known.' I never again alluded to the subject nor did I tolerate in myself the least question leading to the discovery of the privileged Sister. Still I was convinced that I knew her. How often he spoke to me of the marvelous grace that had been vouchsafed to us and I enjoyed too the happiness of noting under his dictation his pious and elevated thoughts on the matter.

"Such are my poor details. They explain the saying of the Curé of Ars uttered many years later speaking of our Community: 'Ah! How the Blessed Virgin loves them! How she watches over them!' These words thrill me with joy. It seems to me that were they known and understood the Seminary would not be large enough to accommodate the number of young souls who would flock to its walls. True they may not be preached from the house-tops. No, we must keep our secret and with Saint Vincent find security in lowliness.

"Many affectionate remembrances to your numerous and fervent family, especially to dear Sister Catherine. Say to her that I rely upon her continued remembrance of me to our Blessed Mother."

This letter from Sister Grand quite dispelled the perplexity of Sister Dufès. With the approval of Superiors a model of the Virgin of the Globe conformable to the directions of the Seer, was executed by the sculptor, Broc Robert. Though the attempt was deemed a success Sister Catherine could not control a disapproving gesture avowing that the Blessed Virgin was more beautiful by far than the representation. However her desire was gratified. The martyrdom of her life had ceased. She might now appear before her Mother in Heaven.

The thought of death seemed ever present to her mind. Her niece accompanied by her two daughters called to see her. To the elder child our Sister gave some little souvenirs of her First Holy Communion.

"Are you not anticipating the event by a whole year?" asked the child's mother,

"My dear child," she rejoined, "I shall not be here next year."

Upon Madame D's. insistence that her aunt was in her normal condition of health, she sweetly replied, "Very well, you do not believe me. Still I repeat, I shall not see 1877."

September eighth came. The long-standing arthritis of the knees, together with heart affection and asthma so debilitated our Blessed Sister that to remain on duty was no longer possible. It will be remarked that this other "bouquet" as she called her sufferings, was presented her on the feast of the Nativity of Our Lady. By November however, her convalescent condition permitted her making a retreat at Rue du Bac. She participated in all the exercises and notwithstanding her age and infirmities knelt like the youngest novice. The only exemption she allowed herself was that during the noonday recreation, she went in search of a former companion of Enghien, at the time a sister of office in the Seminary, to whom she spoke confidentially. One day she requested this Sister to accompany her to the Seminary room where the novices assembled for community devotions. At one end of this room were two pictures by Lecerf, dated 1835, one representing the heart of Saint Vincent, the other the Manifestation of the Blessed Virgin. There she stood in contemplation before the precious souvenirs of her happy privileges. On beholding her countenance so animated, so spiritual, several novices who had unexpectedly entered the room, could not repress their emotion and called out: "That must be the Sister who saw the Blessed Mother." Roused from her ecstasy and visibly annoyed at being discovered, she said: "Very well my Sister," and withdrew with her companion.

BLESSED CATHERINE LABOURÉ

Shortly after the octave of the Immaculate Conception she repeatedly affirmed that she would not live to see the coming year. She intimated too that there would be no need of a hearse for her as she would be taken to Reuilly, adjoining the Hospital of Enghien. These and other predictions were fully realized.

Ten years before her death she said to one of her companions:

"We shall leave Enghien."

"But who told you so, Sister Catherine?"

"I saw in large characters on a grand castle *Hospice d'Enghien.*"

The fact is that on the first of May 1901, the old men of Rue de Picpus took possession of the Castle of Amboise, the property of the late Duke of Aumale. At the entrance was the inscription *Hospice d'Enghien et Orleans.* Sister Catherine had moreover described the very costume to be worn by the future inmates—"the men will be clothed in blue and the women in black" she foretold.

HER DEATH

An interesting anecdote making allusion to a prophecy of our Blessed Sister is related by Rev. Father Baudier of the Society of Jesus in a letter to Father Léon Forestier, Assistant of the Congregation of the Mission at Paris in 1897. It concerned a priest, the Abbé Piau who in the early part of the nineteenth century published various little tracts of devotion, under the signature Abbé P. Vicar General of Evreux. In 1830 he was attached to a corps of almoners under Charles X, and it was in this capacity that he met now and then Sister Catherine. Despite the fact that soon after that date the almonership was surpressed, he still continued to visit Sister Catherine at the Hospital of Enghien. On the occasion of one of these visits he mentioned to Sister Catherine the situation of his personal affairs.

"My Father," she said to him, "go to Switzerland. A mission there awaits you."

That he placed implicit confidence in her words is evidenced by the fact that he set out at once for Switzerland. But did he there find a mission and

did he fulfil it? Yes, a mission awaited him, an
obscure mission, it is true, but one that he nobly
accomplished. He became the Almoner of the
Novitiate of the Sacred Heart, at first at Montet
in Switzerland, later at Kientsheim in Alsace, six
miles from Colmar. After faithfully discharging
these functions for twenty years, he died in Kientsheim in 1857.

"About twenty-seven or twenty-eight years
ago," wrote the Jesuit Father whose testimony we
have quoted, "I was at Kientsheim. The Superioress was Madame Ferdinande Voitot who had
been a novice at Montet. We spoke together of
the Abbé Piau and of the vast amount of good he
effected. In the course of the conversation she
remarked: 'He believed he had a special mission,
because Sister Catherine had directed him saying:
My Father, go to Switzerland. There a mission
awaits you,' "

A priest of the diocese of Paris, the Abbé Olmer,
Almoner of the National Institution for blind children, was instructed by diocesan authority in
1874 to build a church in the locality of Bel Air,

District XII. In 1875 Sister Catherine announced
to the Rev. Abbé that the new church in the
vicinity of the Hospital of Enghien would be dedicated under the title of the Immaculate Conception
and that he would be named Pastor. The title
first selected for the church was that of Saint
Ragonda. This was September 1874. On the
twenty-eighth of March 1877 an ordinance of His
Eminence, Cardinal Gilbert, replaced the first title
by that of the Immaculate Conception and on the
twenty-seventh of September in the same year the
Abbé Olmer was appointed Pastor. In 1909 the
February issue of *La Semaine Religieuse de Paris*
gives room to an article regarding the Rev. Canon
Olmer wherein may be read: "Two years previous
to his nomination he had been saluted with the
title 'Curé of the Immaculate Conception,' by
Sister Catherine Labouré, the privileged Sister of
the Miraculous Medal, though nothing at the time
indicated the choice."

In 1876 the Rev. Father Chevalier, Assistant
of the Congregation of the Mission and Director
of the Daughters of Charity, in view of a new

edition of Father Aladel's "Notice on the Miraculous Medal," which he contemplated publishing, from time to time came to Enghien to confer with the saintly Sister concerning the apparitions. On one occasion the Servant of God declared to him: "When Father Aladel prepared the edition of 1842, I told him he would not publish another and that neither he nor I would live to see a new edition." In fact Father Chevalier's book appeared only in 1878, more than a year after the holy death of Sister Catherine.

Blessed Catherine had at length arrived nigh the term of her mortal life. That hour which would usher her into a blissful eternity was about to strike. It was Sunday December thirty-first. Several attacks of weakness during the day convinced us that it was time to speak to her of receiving the last consolations of religion. She accepted the proposal with deep gratitude and received the Last Sacraments with indescribable tranquillity and happiness.

Some time before this, Sister Catherine had said: "During my agony, I should like to have sixty-three children salute the Blessed Virgin by the invocations which recall her Immaculate Conception, especially the consoling one 'Terror of demons, pray for us.' "

"But," asked a Sister. "are there sixty-three invocations in the litany?"

"You will find them," she replied, "in the Little Office of the Immaculate Conception."

In their desire to comply with her request the Sisters prepared cards containing the several invocations and held them in readiness for the supreme moment. It happened however that on this very Sunday, the eve of the New Year, the children having gone to greet their relatives with the season's wishes, were not available. The Servant of God then asked that the Litany of the Immaculate Conception be recited and that the invocation which causes hell to tremble be thrice repeated.

In the presence of her companions Sister Catherine renewed the Vows of a Daughter of Charity. She then distributed small packages of Miraculous Medals, her little souvenirs to certain designated persons. Several of the old Sisters and some friends of the establishment came to see her for the last time. The sister of office in the Seminary to whom reference has been made above, said to her: "Sister Catherine, you are not going to leave us without saying a word about Blessed Mother?"

Inclining herself toward the sister she said softly: "I may not speak. It is Father Chevalier who is commissioned to do that." Then she added: "The Blessed Virgin is grieved because the great gift bestowed upon the Community of devotion to the Immaculate Conception, is not sufficiently appreciated. Its immense advantages are not understood, and she grieves too because the chaplet is badly recited."

Then her memory transported her to the sanctuary of the apparitions and she remarked: "The Blessed Virgin has promised to grant special graces to those who pray in this chapel, above all an increase of purity, that purity of heart, body and mind which is pure love."

"Are you afraid to die, my dear Sister Catherine?" asked Sister Dufès.

HER DEATH

"Afraid, my Sister, why should I be afraid? I am going to our Lord, to the Blessed Virgin, to Saint Vincent."

When her Superioress confided to her care certain commissions for Heaven, she said: "I am ignorant of the language of Heaven but be assured that your commissions will receive attention."

At four o'clock in the afternoon another attack of faintness gathered her companions around her bed. Yet it was not the final summons. At seven our beloved Sister seemed to be sinking. The Superioress came in haste. With no agony and apparently without suffering, the Servant of God yielded unto Him her pure soul. "Never," declared Sister Dufès, "have I witnessed a death so calm and so sweet."

The death of Sister Catherine was the signal of her triumph. "Sadness by no means swayed our hearts," writes the Superioress. "Not a tear was shed at that eventful moment. An indefinable emotion overpowered us. We felt that we were beside a saint. The veil of humility beneath which

213

she had so long lived was lifted that henceforth we might view only the soul of the privileged child of Heaven." The Sisters of Enghien and Reuilly vied with each other for the honor and gratification of watching during the night near the precious remains. The next day the virginal body of the deceased was carried to the chapel and wreathed round with lilies and roses. And the Sister who in life was scarcely noticed was now gazed upon and invoked by rich and poor, great and lowly, young and old, all eager to place some object of piety in contact with the mortal remains of her on whose brow rested not the pallor of death but the whiteness of alabaster.

But where was such a treasure to be laid away? Her companions could not endure the thought of consigning her to the common burial place of the Community. Yet there was small hope of obtaining the required authorization to preserve her body in their midst. As the Sisters watched beside the remains of their loved Sister, their prayers were not ineffectual. The morning of the second of January as Sister Dufès according to custom rang

214

the four o'clock bell, she distinctly heard these words: "The vault under the chapel at Reuilly."

"That is true," she joyfully said to herself, recollecting that in the erection of the chapel a vault had been constructed which Mother Mazin, then Superioress had put to no use, saying: "It might be of service hereafter."

It was the eve of the funeral. There was no time to lose. The authorization so difficult to secure had not even been solicited. The vault was hastily prepared and the petition supported by influential personages succeeded beyond expectation.

The interment took place January 3, 1877, the feast of Saint Genevieve. After the Mass at ten o'clock a veritable procession was in line from the Hospital of Enghien to the Chapel of Reuilly. Slowly it followed the long garden walk between the two houses. In the lead were the young artisans of the Faubourg Saint Antoine bearing their banner of the Children of Mary. These were followed by the little orphans and the young girls

215

of the various branches of the same sodality. Over two hundred fifty Sisters, the Priests of the Mission and those of the parish immediately preceded the modest casket almost concealed from view under a profusion of lilies and eglantine. No hearse was used, loving hands bore the precious burden, as with measured pace the cortège wended its way to the solemn chant of the *Benedictus*.

At the entrance to the vault the crowd fell back while the Children of Mary greeted the arrival of the body with the significant invocation, "O Mary conceived without sin, pray for us who have recourse to thee." Then the poor whom Sister Catherine had so faithfully served deposited on her tomb a beautiful wreath.

On the very day of the funeral obsequies, Sister Grand whose testimony we have already recorded, sent the following lines to Sister Dufès:

My very dear Sister:

The grace of our Lord be forever with us!

Your thoughtfulness has deeply touched my heart. You were mindful of me at the moment you offered to our Lord a sacrifice that cost much

to your own heart. You have appreciated the bond
which united me to this holy Daughter of Charity,
by giving me without delay intelligence of her
happiness. Truly she could close her eyes to this
world without fear, for the embrace of the Immaculate awaited her and the angels with festive
strains celebrated her entrance into Heaven.

I rejoice in her happiness though in reading the
lines telling of our loss, I could not suppress the
emotion that quite mastered my heart. Good,
holy Sister Catherine! She is safe, the Blessed
Virgin has crowned her devoted servant who so
well kept the secret of her wonderful privileges,
who so well knew how to refer all the glory to
God, while she concealed herself in the obscurity
of silence and the hidden life. What a providence
that during these latter days she spoke with freedom and candor! Her last efforts, her last desires
tended not otherwise than to assure the perpetuity
of the remembrance of the favors of Mary and of
the wonders of which she had been the witness
and the privileged confidante. Indeed the various
utterances during the months that preceded her

217

death seemed to announce that the term of her life was at hand.

Good Sister Catherine! She who had led such a hidden life certainly would not have spoken unless interiorly urged to recall the favor of the apparitions. I have no further details to offer. To Father Chevalier I have imparted whatsoever I could recall. There remains however one circumstance. I refer to the interior preparation for the reception of the precious grace with which she was favored. It appears that for a long time this pure and fervent soul burned with desire to see the Queen of Angels and with holy importunity solicited the signal grace that finally crowned her desires.

I am one with you in sorrow and consolation. If the former has been poignant, the latter is indeed sweet and encouraging. We have a devoted advocate to plead for us with our august Mother, and we have the consoling hope that she will remember, now that she is before the throne of Mary Immaculate, the double family of which she was the treasure.

BLESSED CATHERINE PRAY FOR US

APPENDIX

DECREE

PARISIAN

for the

BEATIFICATION AND CANONIZATION

of the

VENERABLE SERVANT OF GOD

CATHERINE LABOURÉ

of the

SOCIETY OF DAUGHTERS OF CHARITY

On the Question:

Have there been true miracles and have the miracles presented in the case and for the end sought been proved?

Catherine Labouré: this name, which during her life the Venerable concealed a long time under the veil of humility, later became known and revered by the Church at the time of the prodigious expansion throughout the world of the Miraculous Medal which the Immaculate Virgin deigned to confide to Catherine Labouré.

221

APPENDIX

In the school of the Founder of the Company of the Daughters of Charity, as a true Daughter of Saint Vincent de Paul, Catherine devoted herself during nearly the entire course of her community life to the labors of an energetic and toilsome charity at the hospital for poor old men at Paris, where she slept in the Lord, December 31, 1876.

It has been already proclaimed, July 19, 1931, by a Decree of this Sacred Congregation of Rites, that the life of Sister Catherine ennobled by the service of the poor has been truly adorned by her heroic virtues.

But God Himself comes to render illustrious by the glory of miracles, this humble Daughter of Charity. In effect, among several other prodigies attributed to her intercession, the following are two cures which the truly diligent postulators of the Cause have selected as realizing the characteristics of a true miracle.

The first cure occurred at Turin. In this city, on the evening of December 3, 1928, a soldier about twenty-four years of age, Marius Zeme, arrived on a litter at the Grand Military Hospital; he there received Extreme Unction, and shortly after underwent a serious surgical operation. From the beginning, the surgeons and physicians saw clearly

with their eyes, felt with their hands and consequently verified with evidence an acute and purulent case of peritonitis. Of death there could be no
doubt; all hope of a cure was relinquished. The
next day, December 4, Zeme received Holy Viati-
cum, and during December 5 his condition gradually became more serious: death was inevitable
in the opinion of the physicians. Meantime the
Mother of Marius multiplied her prayers to the
Virgin to obtain the cure of the dear patient. The
favor was requested also by a great number of the
sick cared for in the hospital of the Daughters of
Charity. They prayed and begged God explicitly
for a miracle which would be a testimony of the
sanctity of Catherine, dear and faithful servant of
God. Even before the dawn of December 6, the
prayers were answered and health was restored to
dear Marius.

Great were the admiration and astonishment of
the physicians, when several hours later, they declared, contrary to all hope, a change so considera-
ble that there remained no symptoms of peritonitis;
a truly miraculous cure which they recognized, and
in the course of the process, affirmed under oath.
Two expert physicians deposed that at said time
the recovered health continued; and three others
summoned by the Congregation of Rites, attested

APPENDIX

that they also had diagnosed the case before and after the cure, and they proclaimed it a miracle.

Toulouse saw the second miraculous cure. Jean Ribet, a child of six years, was attacked by Pott's disease, clearly revealed by the X-Ray pictures, dated July 1929, as was testified during the process by three attendant physicians. The disease resisted all care and treatment; moreover the condition became worse. At the sight of such a state, in order to obtain of the Virgin the cure of the child, he, with his parents, his grandmother, his brother, united with the Daughters of Charity, began November 19, 1929, a novena to our Lady of the Miraculous Medal, through the intercession of Venerable Catherine, of whom a small relic was placed on the breast of Jean Ribet

November 26, about ten o'clock in the morning, the child suddenly called his mother, who upon her arrival, found him in perfect health. The complete cure and entire restoration of the child are clearly shown by the X-Ray pictures, as affirmed by the attendant physicians, who declare that all that had passed was contrary to the laws of nature. Able physicians attested that the cure is permanent, and three experts also, called by the Congregation of Rites, confirmed the diagnosis before and after the cure, attributing it to a divine miracle.

DECREE

Therefore, all the requisite formalities being complied with, in the presence of the Most Reverend Cardinal Alexander Verde, Ponent or Reporter of the Cause, were held, May 10, 1932, the Antepreparatory Congregation, and on the twelfth of December following, the Preparatory Congregation. Finally, before the general Congregation, convoked for February 7, 1933, in presence of our Holy Father, Pius XI, was proposed by the aforementioned Most Reverend Cardinal, Ponent and Reporter of the Cause, the following question: Has there been a true miracle? Those which are proposed in the case, and for the end sought, are they really proved?

The Most Reverend Cardinals, the Prelates and the Consultors, each in turn and according to his conscience, then expressed his opinion. But the Holy Father, having recommended earnest prayer to obtain of God the grace of greater light, reserved his opinion until later.

At length, the Pope, chose to announce his decision on Septuagesima Monday, February 13, 1933, to mark thus happily the beginning of the twelfth year of his pontificate. Therefore, being assembled, the Most Reverend Cardinals Camille Laurenti, Prefect of the Sacred Congregation of Rites, and Alexander Verde, Ponent or Reporter of the

225

APPENDIX

Cause, being summoned also the Reverend P. Salvatore Natucci, Promoter General of the Faith, and me, the undersigned secretary; having celebrated the Holy Sacrifice of the Mass, the Pope then declared to the audience, that the two aforesaid miracles, proved and accomplished by God, were obtained through the intercession of the Venerable Catherine Labouré, viz: the instantaneous and complete cure of Marius Zeme (serious case of acute and purulent peritonitis), and the child, Jean Ribet (very serious case of Pott's disease).

To attest this declaration, this decree, by order of the Pope himself, is promulgated and inserted in the acts of the Sacred Congregation of Rites, this thirteenth day of February, the year of the Lord, 1933.

CAMILLE, Cardinal Laurenti, *Prefect of the Sacred Congregation of Rites.*

Alphonse CARINCI, *Secretary of the Sacred Congregation of Rites.*

DECREE

PARISIAN CAUSE FOR THE BEATIFICATION AND CANONIZATION OF THE VENERABLE SERVANT OF GOD, CATHERINE LABOURÉ OF THE COMPANY OF DAUGHTERS OF CHARITY.

Decree on the Question: The proof of two miracles and of the virtues being from this time accepted, may we safely proceed with the solemn beatification of the aforesaid Venerable Catherine Labouré?

To aid supernaturally His Church Militant, God, always rich in bounty and our aid in time of tribulation, has been accustomed, from time to time, in the course of ages, to send men of great sanctity, who by the help of grace, apply marvelous remedies adapted to our urgent necessities. Before the increase and spread of heresies He sent to combat them, Doctors armed with the sword of holy doctrine; to the hardness and ferocity of the barbarians and the pagans, God opposes the monks, who by their Christlike sweetness soften their rude hearts; against the thirst after temporal goods He

227

sends the Mendicant Orders, who professing absolute poverty teach by word and example the esteem of heavenly goods; against the innovators of
the sixteenth century, sapping the foundations of
Christian Doctrine, He raises up the Congregations
of the Regular Clergy, who teaching and educating
young souls cause the revival of Christian Society
and of Faith and Morals. Thus in the seventeenth
century, an epoch abounding with error and strife,
God by an all providential gift has given France
and the entire Church, Vincent de Paul, munificent
dispenser of the divine bounty and the intrepid
champion of the Faith of Rome. Vincent, a faithful copy of the Son of God, by his grandeur of
soul, has truly extended the field of charity, embracing by a veritable miracle of beneficent help, all
the human miseries of his time. Behold him making the benefit of his incredible charity felt by the
thousands of human beings who were bending under their miseries and sufferings. For this work,
and for that of time to come, Vincent lives again in
his sons, the Priests of the Mission, and in his
Daughters of Charity, without speaking of the innumerable associations which, like rivulets, flow
from him and possess his spirit.

These Daughters of Charity, we may say, num-
bering some forty thousand, are veritably pure

DECREE

doves springing forth from the Mystical Ark, and before the entire world, astonished and stupified, they continue as messengers of peace, to perform innumerable deeds of charity.

Among the remarkable daughters of this Company, the Venerable Catherine Labouré takes rank by every right. Born in the village of Fain-les-Moutiers, in 1806, raised in the midst of her family in true piety towards God and the Blessed Virgin, Catherine merited from then to be admitted to the Daughters of Charity; announcer of peace, a worker of assiduous benevolence, she was consequently chosen by the Virgin Mary.

Finding herself in Paris, among the little Sisters of the Seminary, Catherine prepared herself in the course of the year 1830 for the religious life of her Community. In the month of July, 1830, first, and then principally on the 27th. of the following November, she enjoyed the marvelous Apparition of the Blessed Virgin Mary, who confided to her the care of having a medal struck. This commission, however, was filled by the director of her conscience; as for herself, during forty-six years she observed most humbly, an inviolable silence, according to the order received concerning the apparitions which she had seen.

With its pious invocations, this medal, on which

APPENDIX

is represented the Virgin all pure, led most effectually the Christian people to profess the dogma of the Immaculate Conception, which was shortly after defined; it commenced then, and yet continues to lavish profusely innumerable graces and astonishing favors of all kinds. And these wonders which God operated by means of that medal, the most pious virgin certainly knew but experienced not the least degree of conceit, loving to be ignored and counted as nothing. The very humble employments which obedience confided to her, were filled by Catherine during her entire life, a life unknown to man; she preserved with care that simplicity and most ardent charity which were recommended to her by the doctrine and the precepts of her father, Saint Vincent.

As all the glory of the daughter of the King is within (Psalm 44), so the holiness of the life of Catherine was all and always interior, and until her death she hid herself under the protection of the most profound humility. But scarcely had Catherine departed for God, December 31, 1876, than her virtues were everywhere and abundantly manifested. That is why, Pius X, of holy memory, in 1907, ordered the introduction of the Cause of this Servant of God. On July 19, 1931, on the feast of Saint Vincent de Paul, His Holiness, Pius XI

DECREE

recognized and proclaimed the heroic virtues of Catherine, and on the 13th. of February of this year, 1933, a decree of this Congregation of Rites, approved by the Pope, declared and approved the two cures presented as true miracles.

The way was then open for the Beatification. But now our laws require at the last the discussion of the following question: the proof of two miracles and of the virtues being from this time accepted, may we safely proceed with the solemn beatification of the aforesaid Venerable? The Most Reverend Cardinal Alexander Verde, Ponent or Reporter of this Cause, in the General Congregation of Rites, held February 25, 1933, proposed this question, to which all the Most Reverend Cardinals, the Prelates in charge, and the Fathers Consultors gave an affirmative response. The Pope, nevertheless deferred the pronouncement of his judgement until the twelfth of March, the second Sunday of Lent, when the Gospel of the day presents to us the Transfiguration of Christ, the form and model of the future glorification of the elect.

In the end His Holiness summoned the Most Reverend Cardinals of this Sacred Congregation of Rites, Camille Laurenti, Prefect, and Alexander Verde, Ponent and Reporter of the Cause, and also called Reverend P. Salvator Natucci, Promoter

APPENDIX

General of the Faith, and me, the undersigned secretary; and after having celebrated the Holy Mysteries, notified us that, in all surety, we might proceed with the solemn beatification of the Venerable Servant of God, Catherine Labouré.

The Pope, further declared that the decree should be published and inserted in the Acts of this Sacred Congregation of Rites, and ordained that under the seal of the Fisherman, the Apostolic Letters be sent for the solemnities of the beatification to be celebrated, at the time desired, in the Basilica of the Vatican.

This twelfth of March of the year of our Lord 1933.

Camille LAURENTI,

Prefect of the Sacred Congregation of Rites.

Alphonse CARINCI,

Secretary of the Sacred Congregation of Rites.

RELIQUARY CONTAINING THE HEART OF BLESSED
CATHERINE LABOURÉ

RELIQUARY CONTAINING THE HEART
OF BLESSED CATHERINE LABOURÉ

This reliquary, the artistic creation of Mr. Mel-
lerio, was given to the House of Reuilly, where
Blessed Catherine spent her Community life.

Her heart, sharing the perfect state of preservation of her entire body, was enclosed in this reliquary carved from purest rock crystal and borne
by two angels in an attitude of prayer.

O humble Sister Catherine, thou didst understand
That pure and simple hearts the gifts of Heaven
command;
Thy heart, Which from Death's withering finger
found release,
Like to our Savior and to her who gave Him birth,
Spent all its love on God's forsaken poor on earth,
In recollection deep, in silence, and in peace.

Behold thy heart, now held aloft by hands angelic!
A touching symbolism frames the holy relic,
Encased within a crystal pure, whose clarity
Becomes its fitting rival,---'tis a virgin shrine
Embellished by a lily fair, of chaste design,
Caressing thy pure heart, O Sister of Charity!

EXHUMATION

of the

BODY

of

BLESSED CATHERINE LABOURÉ

Fifty-six years in the obscurity of the grave rested the body of Catherine Labouré, and then, following the announcement of her beatification, March 21, 1933, was decided upon for the exhumation of the body. A few favored ones assembled at the vault, eager, expectant, yet with mingled feelings of hope and fear as to the outcome. Would her body like that of the Little Flower of Jesus be nothing but dust, or would it be like that of Ozanam, a mass of corruption and worms? On the preceding Friday the vault had been unsealed and was found dry; this was very encouraging. The plan was to open the coffin at Reuilly, then the remains, if there were any, were to be placed in a new casket and sent to the Mother House. It was extremely difficult to raise the coffins—for in France the laws are stringent about burying in private vaults. The outer coffin was of wood and to it was affixed a heart-

Ecclesiastical and Medical Delegation at the
Exhumation

EXHUMATION

shaped, steel plate, bearing the age, the name and
the date of interment.   It was falling to pieces and
had to be taken out in sections.   The second coffin
was of lead and consequently perfectly preserved.
With the greatest difficulty it was lifted from the
place where it fitted exactly and where it had rested
for many years.   It was carried to Reuilly where,
after all necessary precautions had been taken, it
was opened with all solemnity.

An altar had been erected in the room where the
casket was to be opened, and large white enameled
tables bearing everything which might be needed
were in readiness.   After oaths had been taken,
the formula of Excommunication read against any
who should change what was found in the coffin,
the undertaker cut the lid of the leaden coffin, lifted
it off, and disclosed the under coffin of wood really
quite well preserved.   The moment was tense as
the physician lifted the sheet which covered the
remains of the holy Sister and discovered the body
intact.   Everyone was in admiration at the wonderful state of preservation.   "The hands", writes an
eye witness, "had slipped towards the side, but
were white and natural looking.   The cord of the
chaplet had decayed and the beads were loose in
the coffin.   The skin on the face had the appearance of parchment, but was entire.   The eyes and

the mouth were closed." Two old ladies, who live at Reuilly and who knew Sister Catherine, were present at the exhumation and when they saw the body they said: "Just like Sister Catherine." Did Providence reward her forty-six years of the hidden life by this miraculous preservation? She who was scarcely known in life was easily recognized after fifty-six years in the grave!

In order to avoid a second handling of the body, it was decided to transfer it at once to the Mother House where the formal examination was to take place on the following day in the presence of the Cardinal and the Promoter of the Faith. Truly the promise of our Lord to the humble was fulfilled in this homecoming, for humility was indeed glorified! By the time the hearse arrived at the Mother House, a double row of Sisters was at the front entrance; following the line of cornettes and near the chapel were priests and novices from Saint Lazare, sons of Saint Vincent de Paul, all bearing lighted candles. In the corridor adjoining the chapel was a double row of Sisters of the Seminary, novices, such as Sister Labouré had been at the time of the Apparitions. There was no ceremony, except the chanting of the "Libera" by the Novices of Saint Lazare, as the heavy leaden casket, covered with a white silk pall on which were embroidered the medal and its reverse, was carried between the double lines of the Sons and Daughters of Saint Vincent de Paul.

At ten o'clock on the following morning there was a solemn examination of the relics of Sister Catherine. When the body had been transferred from the room in which it had been placed, the seal of the room having been broken by a Canon, Promoter of the Faith, the Cardinal said a few words on the honor Sister Catherine had brought to her Community by her humble, hidden life. Then the Canon read the formula of excommunication against anyone who would touch the body without the requisite authority. The undertaker removed the lid, and the body was disclosed to view. The account by one present states: "It had changed somewhat as the light and air had caused the flesh to become discolored. The habit was perfect; the collar and cornette were very yellow. The face was almost black but the features were discernable. There was nothing of the ghastly grinning skeleton and whilst one felt in the presence of death, there was no horror in it. One felt like saying, "Oh grave, where is thy victory; oh death, where is thy sting!"

In the afternoon the operation was held during which the doctors removed the relics. First the

APPENDIX

heart was removed. This is to be given to Reuilly.
Two large bones, one for Rome, and one for the
Cathedral were taken, and after that several ribs,
etc. The body was then wound in immaculate
white, after which it was again wound with red
ribbon and sealed officially here and there by the
Canon of the Cathedral. Articles of piety which
had touched the relics were once more applied to
the covered body. At four o'clock the remains
were carried through the living hedge of Sisters,
Priests and Novices to the room where they rested
until the Beatification on May 28. All united in
the singing of the Magnificat, a hymn of triumph
indeed for the humble, hidden Sister Catherine.

After the Beatification, the relics were placed in a
beautiful shrine under the altar of the Virgin Most
Powerful, the place of the Apparition of November
27, 1830. Is there not in this glorification of
Mary's lowly instrument an assurance of continued
fulfilment of our Blessed Mother's promise, since
our Blessed Sister's mortal remains have been
brought intact to the foot of the chosen shrine? Let
us repair in spirit at least to that sanctuary of the
Immaculate Mary, hearkening anew to her plea:

"Come to the foot of this altar. Here graces
will be showered upon you and upon all who ask
for them."

238

CARRYING THE REMAINS OF BLESSED CATHERINE ACROSS
THE COURTYARD OF THE MOTHER HOUSE

EXHUMATION

The doctor who conducted the examination of the relics entered this record relative to the Exhumation of the Body of Blessed Catherine Labouré: Tuesday, March 21, 1933 at Rue de Reuilly, we were able to establish the following facts:

The outer coffin of dark wood was practically totally decayed. The leaden shell was partly intact with the exception of a fissure on the left, at the head of the coffin, extending to the level of the third lower vertical soldering; no liquid issued through the perforations made in the lead at this time.

The lead being cut away it was easy to see that the pine coffin remained intact. On opening this we found a grayish mass of sawdust which had taken the form of the body; on the surface of this were some evidences of mould; but there was no putrefaction, simply a slightly acid odor.

After carefully removing the sawdust by hand the winding sheet could be seen; it was intact, slightly damp and could easily be unfolded.

The body was then cleared of all encumbrance. It seemed to be perfectly preserved in clothing which had kept its color and normal consistency.

The cornette had remained over the face and this with the weight of the winding sheet and sawdust caused the nose to be flattened.

APPENDIX

The hands and the face were of a pinkish color slightly tinged with brown, but intact. Two fingers of the left hand were somewhat blackened, but we quickly perceived that this dark color was not due to necrosis of the tissue but to the dye of the habit which had faded on to the hand on the side of the crack in the leaden coffin. These facts being ascertained we replaced the sheet and sealed the coffin for the transporting of the body.

Wednesday, March 22, 140 Rue du Bac.—The body was carefully taken out of the coffin and placed on a long table.

The face on account of its first contact with the air had slightly darkened since the day before; the clothing perfectly preserved was carefully removed. It is well to note that on the left side of the body, the side in contact with the crack in the leaden coffin, the clothing was a little damp, and some parts of the body (the left arm and shoulder) had undergone a slight attrition.

The skin there was a little swollen, hardened, and showed on its surface some whitish, limelike deposits. In examining the body we noticed the perfect suppleness of the arms and legs. These members have merely undergone a slight mumification. The skin throughout was intact and like parchment. The muscles were preserved; we could easily dissect them in a study of anatomy.

We cut the sternum on the median line. The bone showed a cartilaginous, elastic consistency and was easily cut by the surgeon's knife. The thoracic cavity being opened it was easy for us to remove the heart. It was much shrunken but it had kept its shape. We could easily see within it the little fibrous cords, remains of the valves and muscles. We also took out a number of the ribs and the clavicle. We disjointed the arms—these two will be conserved apart. The two knee caps were taken out. The finger and toe nails were in perfect condition. The hair remained attached to the scalp.

The eyes were in the orbits; the eyelids half closed; we were able to state that the ball though fallen and shrunken existed in its entirety, and even the color, bluish gray, of the iris still remained. The ears were intact.

To insure the preservation of the body we injected a solution of formaldihyde, glycerine and carbolic acid.

Paris, March 25, 1933.

Dr. Robert DIDIER,
Community Surgeon,
Knight of the Legion of Honor,
Knight of St. Gregory the Great

CPSIA information can be obtained
at www.ICGtesting.com
Printed in the USA
BVHW031922080919

557870BV00003B/7/P

9 781164 497608